49.95

Campaigns and Conscience

**Recent Titles in the Praeger Series
in Political Communication**
Robert E. Denton, Jr., General Editor

Broadcasting Propaganda: International Radio Broadcasting and the
Construction of Political Reality
Philo C. Wasburn

Enacting the Presidency: Political Argument, Presidential Debates, and
Presidential Character
Edward A. Hinck

Citizens, Political Communication and Interest Groups: Environmental
Organizations in Canada and the United States
John C. Pierce, Mary Ann E. Steger, Brent S. Steel, and Nicholas P. Lovric

Media and Public Policy
Edited by Robert J. Spitzer

Cold War Analytical Structures and the Post Post-War World
Cori E. Dauber

American Rhetoric and the Vietnam War
J. Justin Gustainis

The Inaugural Addresses of Twentieth-Century American Presidents
Edited by Halford Ryan

Studies in Media and the Persian Gulf War
Edited by Robert E. Denton, Jr.

The Modern Presidency and Crisis Rhetoric
Edited by Amos Kiewe

Governmental Commission Communication
Christine M. Miller and Bruce C. McKinney, editors

The Presidential Campaign Film: A Critical History
Joanne Morreale

High-Tech Campaigns: Computer Technology in Political
Communication
Gary W. Selnow

Rhetorical Studies of National Political Debates: 1960–1992
Robert V. Friedenberg, editor

CAMPAIGNS AND CONSCIENCE

The Ethics of Political Journalism

Philip Seib

Praeger Series in Political Communication

 PRAEGER

Westport, Connecticut
London

Library of Congress Cataloging-in-Publication Data

Seib, Philip M.
    Campaigns and conscience : the ethics of political journalism /
Philip Seib.
        p. cm.—(Praeger series in political communication, ISSN
1062–5623)
    Includes bibliographical references and index.
    ISBN 0–275–94623–1 (alk. paper).—ISBN 0–275–94624–X (pbk. :
alk. paper)
    1. Journalism—Political aspects—United States. 2. Journalistic
ethics. 3. Press and politics—United States. 4. Electioneering—
United States. I. Title. II. Series.
PN4781.S45 1994
174'.9097—dc20   93–37023

British Library Cataloguing in Publication Data is available.

Library of Congress Catalog Card Number: 93–37023
ISBN: 0–275–94623–1
    0–275–94624–X (pbk.)
ISSN: 1062–5623

First published in 1994

Praeger Publishers, 88 Post Road West, Westport, CT 06881
An imprint of Greenwood Publishing Group, Inc.

Printed in the United States of America

The paper used in this book complies with the
Permanent Paper Standard issued by the National
Information Standards Organization (Z39.48–1984).

10 9 8 7 6 5 4 3 2 1

for Christine

Contents

Series Foreword *by Robert E. Denton, Jr.*   ix

Preface   xi

1   What's at Stake   1

2   Journalists' Competence   21

3   The Character Issue   41

4   On the Bus   59

5   Campaign Advertising   91

6   Polls, Projections, and Endorsements   105

7   Covering the News Media   121

8   The Future . . . and Some Suggestions   133

Notes   143

Bibliography   151

Index   157

Series Foreword

Those of us in the field of communication studies have long believed that communication comes before all other fields of inquiry. In several other forums I have argued that the essence of politics is "talk" or human interaction.[1] Such interaction may be formal or informal, verbal or non-verbal, public or private, but it is always persuasive, forcing us consciously or subconsciously to interpret, to evaluate, and to act. Communication is the vehicle for human action.

From this perspective, it is not surprising that Aristotle recognized the natural kinship of politics and communication in his *Politics* and *Rhetoric*. In the former, he establishes that humans are "political beings [who] alone of the animals [are] furnished with the faculty of language."[2] In the latter, he begins his systematic analysis of discourse by proclaiming that "rhetorical study, in its strict sense, is concerned with the modes of persuasion."[3] Thus, it was recognized over 2,300 years ago that politics and communication go hand in hand because they are essential parts of human nature.

In 1981, Dan Nimmo and Keith Sanders proclaimed that political communication was an emerging field.[4] Although its origin, as noted, dates back centuries, a "self-consciously cross-disciplinary" focus began in the late 1950s. Thousands of books and articles later, colleges and universities offer a variety of graduate and undergraduate coursework in the area in such diverse departments as communication, mass communication, journalism, political science, and sociology.[5] In Nimmo and Sanders's early assessment, the "key areas of inquiry" included rhetorical analysis, propaganda analysis, attitude change studies, voting studies, government and the news media, functional and systems analyses, technological changes, media technologies, campaign techniques, and research techniques.[6] In a survey of the state of the field in 1983, the same authors plus Lynda Kaid found additional, more specific areas of concerns such as the presidency, political polls, public opinion, debates, and advertising, to name a few.[7] They also noted a shift away from the rather strict behavioral approach they had seen at the time of the first study.

In the early 1990s, Dan Nimmo and David Swanson asserted that "political communication has developed some identity as a more or less distinct domain of scholarly work."[8] The scope and concerns of the area have further expanded to include critical theories and cultural studies. While there is no precise definition, method, or disciplinary home of the area of inquiry, its primary domain is the role, processes, and effects of communication within the context of politics broadly defined.

In 1985, the editors of *Political Communication Yearbook: 1984* noted that "more things are happening in the study, teaching, and practice of political communication than can be captured within the space limitations of the relatively few publications available."[9] In addition, they argued that the backgrounds of "those involved in the field [are] so varied and pluralist in outlook and approach, . . . it [is] a mistake to adhere slavishly to any set format in shaping the content."[10] And more recently, Swanson and Nimmo called for "ways of overcoming the unhappy consequences of fragmentation within a framework that respects, encourages, and benefits from diverse scholarly commitments, agendas, and approaches."[11]

In agreement with these assessments of the area and with gentle encouragement, in 1988 Praeger Publishers established the series entitled "Praeger Studies in Political Communication." The series is open to all qualitative and quantitative methodologies as well as contemporary and historical studies. The key to characterizing the studies in the series is the focus on communication variables or activities within a political context or dimension. Scholars from the disciplines of communication, history, political science, and sociology have participated in the series.

I am, without shame or modesty, a fan of the series. The joy of serving as its editor is in participating in the dialogue of the field of political communication and in reading the contributors' works. I invite you to join me.

Robert E. Denton, Jr.

Preface

The first reaction is always the same: "You're writing a book about the ethics of political journalism? How long is it going to be—ten pages?"

That's funny . . . and sad. Political journalism is important. So are its practitioners' ethics.

For a journalist, being assigned to a major political campaign is just about as good as being sent to cover a war.

News is always being made; adrenaline is always flowing. Your stories will often make page 1 or the top of a newscast. You're part of an elite band, a witness to history, a star. And, ideally, you're giving your constituents—those who read or see or hear you—what they need to know to cast an informed vote.

That's the romanticized version. Reality is often less glorious: eighteen-hour workdays and seven-day workweeks; bumpy airplane rides and lumpy motel mattresses; searching for facts in candidates' speeches and looking for truth in the barrage of charges and countercharges.

The one constant is the public's need for information. However arduous or unsavory the job may become, you're still obligated to let your audience know what's going on, and to do so honestly and thoroughly.

Political news gathering differs from much else in journalism because of the dynamic tension that exists between reporters and those they cover. Most of the daily events that constitute news—such as the spectacular disaster or the grisly crime—demand certain reportorial enterprise and insight, but the subjects of those stories usually don't fight back and try to shape the news product the way politicians do.

Besides this tension, a mutual dependence exists between the politician and the journalist—one wanting to be covered, the other wanting something to cover. This can work against the interests of the third party in the process: the voter and news consumer.

The politician-journalist relationship is both adversarial and symbiotic. It provides the backdrop for diverse ethical issues with which political journalists must grapple.

This book has two principal purposes: to identify these ethical problems and to suggest some ways to resolve them, fostering a more responsible and more informative political journalism.

Chapter 1 outlines the scope of these issues, discussing the influence of political coverage and the struggle journalists must wage to keep that coverage honest and accurate. Politicians' strategy is increasingly devoted to shaping news reports in ways that will most favor them. An unwary correspondent will often be victimized by this manipulation.

Chapter 2 addresses what a political journalist should know. A reporter's fundamental ethical responsibility is not to be an idiot. Competence is the product of much hard work; the journalist should know at least as much about issues and strategies as the politicians do. This knowledge will be the foundation for some of the most important news judgments: deciding what to cover and what to ignore.

This chapter also asks a difficult question: Should the journalist report the news or the truth? Sometimes they're not the same. For instance, if a candidate gives a speech, that's news. But suppose the speech is filled with inaccuracy and distortion. Should reporters just report the *news*—the speech as given—and leave rebuttal to another politician, or should journalists take it upon themselves to present the *truth* in contrast to the speech content? Underlying such matters is finding a theoretical and practical definition of *fairness*.

Chapter 3 looks at the "character" issue, examining its evolution since George Washington's time and looking at recent cases involving Gary Hart, Bill Clinton, and others. Some guidelines are suggested about how much privacy should be granted to politicians and about circumstances that justify invading this privacy.

In Chapter 4, the spotlight turns to the daily grind of campaigning. Few news consumers know what goes into the reports that appear in their morning paper or on the evening newscast. This chapter provides a look at campaign life "on the bus" and ethical problems that arise there. Among this chapter's topics are pack journalism, relationships between journalists and those they cover, and how reporters handicap a "horse race" that has elective office awaiting the winner.

Chapter 5 offers suggestions about a relatively new element of political reporting—analyzing candidates' advertising. Because politicians rely so heavily on ads to reach voters, their spots are no less deserving of coverage than are speeches and other campaign events. In addition to surveying the history of political advertising, this chapter reviews "truth testing" for ads—an evolving journalistic practice that requires careful research and formatting if voters are to be well served.

In Chapter 6, the value and dangers of opinion polling are discussed. Polls offer snapshots of the public's mood. As such, they're a useful part of the mosaic of campaign reporting. But they often are overemphasized and unduly influence other aspects of coverage. Also, journalists must beware of polls designed to produce propaganda rather than honest data.

Related to these polling problems are Election Night projections. The best-known controversy involves premature predictions that might affect voter turnout. Decisions must be made about this culmination of campaign coverage. In the competitive rush to report vote returns, do news organizations ignore the impact their coverage might have on voter behavior and electoral outcomes?

Also covered in this chapter is the editorial endorsement. Many news organizations—principally print—endorse candidates. Those decisions and the relationship between editorial stance and news coverage often are not understood by the public. The procedure should not be a mystery; news consumers have a right to know how it works.

Chapter 7 examines how the news media cover the news media. No other institution of comparable power escapes press scrutiny. Despite the peril of conflicting interests and the awkwardness of introspection, more ways should be found for journalists to report about their profession.

In Chapter 8, the prospects for ethical political journalism are evaluated. For one thing, evolving news technologies necessitate evolving news ethics. These changes must be matched by an increasingly sophisticated appreciation of journalists' responsibilities. Without news professionals understanding what's at stake, ethics never will be given appropriate attention. In political journalism, knowledge of ethics is just as important as knowledge of politics.

The tone throughout much of this book is hortatory. I did that purposely, trying to stimulate debate. When I write, "Journalists should do such and such," I hope readers will challenge, argue, and—most important—think.

This book is designed to be of particular assistance to students of journalism. They can become the collective conscience of the profession, shaping its standards and its future. Those who go on to careers as scholars or as reporters, editors, producers, and other news professionals should have firm grounding in the ethical principles of delivering the news to the public.

Only if they do, will the essential role of the political journalist be performed as it should be.

Many thanks are owed to many people for help and inspiration they provided while I was writing this book:

— My colleagues at Southern Methodist University—especially Darwin Payne, Rita Whillock, and John Gartley—have been unfailingly supportive.

— My energetic research assistant, Vanessa Polak, found even the most obscure materials and delivered them to me so thoroughly organized and annotated that writing sometimes was fun.

— My journalistic colleagues at WFAA Television and the *Dallas Morning News*, with whom I have covered campaigns and endlessly talked about politics and journalism, kept me in touch with the "real world." Among the many are Marty Haag, John Miller, Doug Fox, Cinny Kennard, Carolyn Barta, and Rena Pederson. Other journalist friends, such as David Broder and Mary McGrory, have consistently proved that political journalism and ethics are compatible; I value having known them for so many years. My parents, Charles and Shirley Seib, both far better journalists than I am, also recognized the importance of high standards in their careers. And my wife, Christine Wicker—yet another journalist—has helped and inspired me in so many ways that I'll just say, "Thanks."

Chapter One

What's at Stake

Political journalism matters.

That's not just a reporter's ego speaking. It's a hard fact about how the political system works.

Politicians' words and deeds earn few votes unless the public knows about them. Issues may seem obscure and unimportant unless news stories explain their significance. And, from another perspective, candidates can learn much about the electorate by monitoring what news organizations report, especially local media.

In most top-of-the-ballot races, candidates have no choice but to rely on news coverage to reach voters. More than 100 million Americans go to the polls in a presidential election. Bus tours and whistle-stop train trips have their quaint appeal, and, as was the case for Bill Clinton in 1992, this kind of campaigning can forge a symbolic bond with voters and set the tone for a candidacy. But such in-person campaigning will never get a candidate in touch with the massive number of voters he or she needs to win.

Through advertising, a candidate can try to circumvent news coverage, but only the rare, free-spending billionaire—Ross Perots don't materialize often—can afford to purchase exposure comparable with what the news media offer. Even when a candidate has an unlimited bankroll, voters will look to news reports to provide many of the pieces in the jigsaw puzzle of politics.

The political dynamic that eventually generates a voting decision is the product of a tripartite system (or, in less erudite but perhaps more accurate terms, a three-headed monster):

- The *candidate* addresses subtle and not-so-subtle solicitations to the voter. Some are direct—such as television ads and mailings—and some are filtered by the news media.

- The *journalist*, with varying degrees of diligence and imagination, gathers "news"—about topics ranging from nuclear arms control to a candidate's collegiate marijuana smoking—from politicos and other sources and delivers it to the voter.
- The *voter* selects pieces of the flotsam drifting by on this flood of information and uses them to construct opinions and ultimately ballot decisions.

Mystery surrounds this selection and construction process. Which pieces are relied on and which are ignored? If a foolproof answer to that question existed, politicians and reporters could save themselves a lot of trouble. But despite having at hand reams of sophisticated survey data, no sensible person involved in politics has come up with a conclusive answer.

The relationship among these three players—vote seeker, journalist, and voter—is symbiotic. The candidate needs mechanisms to communicate messages, and then needs votes. The journalist needs information from the politician and needs to garner and maintain a news-consuming audience (as measured by rating points and circulation figures). The voter needs input from the other two, to help decide whom to trust and whom to support.

Journalists have ethical obligations to both of the other members of this troika. To the politician is owed the duty to report fairly and comprehensively, recognizing the essential role of the messenger.

But it is to the voter that the journalist has the highest responsibility. Principal allegiance must be to the news consumer rather than the news source. At the heart of this obligation is defining and supplying what the voters require in making their political decisions.

This is a complex task because "the voters" comprise a vast, amorphous mass in which are clustered hopes and fears and wants and needs that have almost as many variations as the electorate has faces.

Journalists must resist the allure of trying to be all things to all people (leaving that to the politicians) and just try to construct a sprawling, helpful framework on which voters can base their choices. This incorporates three generalized tasks:

- Influencing the issues agenda
- Reporting candidates' positions, claims, and charges
- Resisting manipulation

SPOTLIGHTING ISSUES

Early in the campaign season, news organizations help define the issues agenda that will fuel public debate. This does not usurp the politicians' responsibility, nor does it overstep ethical bounds. Leaving agenda-setting solely to the candidates would mean that some important but complicated issues probably would be given low priority or ignored altogether. Many politicians tend to address only those issues they think are safe vote-winners. They shy away from those that might involve complexity or controversy.

This process can be approached in several ways. Knowledgeable journalists can easily devise a basic issues list in a brainstorming session. But an agenda more representative of public concerns might be created by using survey research. That's how politicians find out what the public thinks is important; news organizations can do the same thing.

In 1992, the Charlotte (N.C.) *Observer* decided to gear its political coverage to the substantive matters voters wanted to know about, rather than to the most sensational incident of the moment. Using focus groups and surveys, the newspaper made an extraordinary effort to become truly the agent of its readers.

That meant candidates' health care plans received coverage at the expense of Gennifer Flowers's lurid tales about her purported relationship with Bill Clinton. With tabloid-style journalism much in vogue at times during that campaign, *Observer* editors may have felt out of step with their colleagues, but over the long haul, they delivered a more thoughtful and more useful news product.

Emphasis was placed on making readers feel they were participants in the coverage, not merely passive recipients of the news product. As Elizabeth Kolbert reported in the *New York Times*: "Acting on the same theory that seems to work so well for Phil Donahue—the more the audience gets to participate, the more they like the show—editors at the *Observer* spent much of the primary season looking for new ways to involve readers."[1] For example, *Observer* readers were invited to submit questions for reporters to ask candidates and sometimes were invited to grill the candidates themselves.

The resulting coverage *was* different. "The paper did not commission a single poll to find out which candidates were leading in public opinion. Articles on the sniping between the candidates, common in other papers, were kept to a minimum."[2]

In Kansas, the *Wichita Eagle* has run a similar program since 1990. It, too, emphasizes issues and reader involvement.[3] These projects haven't turned the political world upside down, but they represent incremental change. Presumably, similar experiments will follow elsewhere.

Television networks and stations also use focus groups to get a sense of voters' priorities and their reactions to candidates. This helps break through the insularity that can hamper journalists who spend most of their time talking to those they cover and to other journalists. Sometimes the "real world" is a foreign place. The focus group members may not possess any unique wisdom, but at least their voices are different from those the journalists usually hear. Also, their opinions may differ from views of the "experts" on whom journalists heavily rely.

Like much else, however, using focus groups can slip into gimmickry. For instance, at the end of the 1992 campaign, ABC could not resist asking—with dramatic buildup worthy of a high-stakes quiz show—a handful of "undecided" voters from its focus groups about how they were going to vote. These revelations—brought to millions live on the network's evening newscast—were neither newsworthy nor scientifically valid as indicators of how the following Tuesday's vote would go. When that kind of question is asked, a large sampling of voters should be queried. Presumably, however, the pronouncements were judged to be "good TV" and so were deemed worthy of being inflicted on viewers.

Featuring these individual voting decisions also shifted the purpose of focus groups away from defining substantive issues and to playing "horse race" journalism—who's ahead, who's coming from behind, and so forth (discussed in Chapter 4). That temptation remains hard to resist.

Any trivializing of agenda-setting is unfortunate, because the news media have the opportunity and responsibility to insist on an issues debate that is broader than the politicians might want. Topics that candidates would prefer to ignore can be pushed into the public's consciousness.

A foreign policy example occurred amid the postwar chaos in Iraq in 1991. Hundreds of thousands of Kurds were being driven into Turkey and Iran by Saddam Hussein. Facing virtual genocide from illness and starvation, these enemies of America's enemy were being abandoned because helping them would serve "no strategic purpose" and because protracting U.S. military involvement might tarnish the luster of the Bush administration's Gulf War triumph.

Then news coverage of the Kurds' plight began to intensify. The first wave came in editorials and op ed columns. White House sources smugly announced that these could and would be ignored. The stakes rose when *Newsweek* ran a cover photograph of a sad-looking Kurdish child with this headline, referring to President Bush: " 'Why Won't He Help Us?' " That at least elicited a presidential acknowledgment that the Kurds needed aid. Then vivid television pictures brought the Kurds' suffering to the attention of even more Americans. These pictures led Bush to send Secretary of State James Baker to the Turkey-Iraq border and then to deploy American troops to help protect Kurdish refugee camps against Iraqi attacks.

According to journalist Daniel Schorr,

Within a two-week period, the president had been forced, under the impact of what Americans and Europeans were seeing on television, to reconsider his hasty withdrawal of troops from Iraq. As though to acknowledge this, Mr. Bush told a news conference on April 16, "No one can see the pictures or hear the accounts of this human suffering—men, women, and, most painfully of all, children—and not be deeply moved."[4]

This press influence is not limited to geopolitical catastrophes. On a regular basis, news organizations can amplify the voices of those who often are not heard—minority group members, the physically handicapped, the mentally ill, and others who lack political clout. In doing so, journalists serve as lobbyists for those whom politicians might otherwise forget. If the news media didn't force these concerns onto the issues agenda, they'd likely never get there on their own.

COVERING THE CANDIDATES

Beyond defining what the issues are, news organizations report where candidates stand on those issues. Sometimes the simplest formats are the most useful. On some issues, a side-by-side checklist comparison works well. For instance, if the issue is "Waiting period before handgun purchases," a graphic on the newspaper page or television screen can list the candidates and have "For" or "Against" by their names. Even certain aspects of complex issues such as capital gains tax reform can be shaped to fit this format. But when doing so, the compressed positions demanded by the chart layout should be reinflated in companion stories that treat the topics with appropriate thoroughness.

With an audience increasingly accustomed to visual presentation of news, format is important, but not to the exclusion of other concerns. Conciseness is fine, but policy positions should not be simplified to the point of meaninglessness.

To preserve context, a candidate's position on any given issue should be addressed on three levels: what the candidate wants to do; whether it is doable; and, if done, what its impact will be.

By itself, the first doesn't mean much, and journalists shouldn't be satisfied to report it alone. For example, in a big city mayor's race, when candidates claim to be determined to "wipe out the scourge of drug abuse," reporting their good intentions isn't enough. Journalists press for specifics and analyze their practicality. For instance, if a candidate's formula is based on doubling the size of the police force, plenty of questions need to be asked: How much will it cost? How will this affect local taxes? Where will all these new police officers come from? What, exactly, will they do? Do they have a realistic chance of reducing drug traffic, or will they merely become an army of occupation in parts of the city? What precedents exist elsewhere?

The list goes on. Not every conceivable question the public might have can be answered, but the more the candidate emphasizes this issue and the more extravagant his or her claims become, the more extensive the reporting should be.

This journalistic counterbalance is especially important when candidates shift from issues to accusations. Reporting charges—even when they're answered by an opponent—always involves many ethical risks. Sometimes allegations center on an opponent's public record; sometimes the subject is personal conduct. Sometimes the charges are explicit; sometimes they're implied; sometimes they're a mixture. Whatever the specifics, in the thrust and parry of attack politics, the public often has difficulty deciding whom to believe. The press is an essential referee.

The 1992 presidential campaign offered plenty of examples of this. For instance, George Bush said a Clinton administration would impose such rigorous environmental standards on the automobile industry that "every autoworker in the country will be out of work." Clinton said that was nonsense (and Bush himself later dismissed it as campaign puffery), but the voter doesn't know whose story is closer to the truth. Similarly, when Ross Perot told his tales about Republican dirty tricksters targeting his family, prompt denials came from the White House. Once again, the voter—whether intrigued, horrified, or amused by this story—needed some help in hunting for the truth.

In the auto industry case, reporters could dig through the public pronouncements of Bill Clinton and Al Gore and present their findings. Voters could then make an informed judgment about Bush's contention. The Perot story was more difficult to address, because no hard evidence existed to prove or disprove the charges. But in both instances, news reports were a dispassionate, stabilizing influence, calming some voters' fears and keeping debate from progressing beyond shrillness into hysteria. Most important, news coverage gives truth a chance to float to the surface.

As these cases indicate, the public must not expect news media to resolve every campaign controversy. Journalists, too, must accept this. Their ethical responsibility is to provide information—as thoroughly verified as is possible—that will illuminate political debate and give news consumers additional tools they may use in building their voting decisions. That might not be journalistic perfection, but it is realistic.

AVOIDING MANIPULATION

As journalists work toward this goal, they encounter obstructions carefully engineered by politicians. The pols know that voters distinguish between propaganda and journalism. The message a candidate delivers in a TV ad is less credible than the same message incorporated in a TV news story. So politicians want to manipulate news coverage to make it serve their interests in much the same way advertising does.

This process will be explained in detail in Chapter 4. For now, a few recent examples will suffice.

During the 1988 presidential race, the Bush campaign—featuring hard-nosed professionals such as strategist Lee Atwater and media tactician Roger Ailes—shaped the content and tone of much news coverage. They got away with this mainly because few journalists did anything more than follow wherever the pols led and publish whatever was said. Rare were objections to the intellectually vapid campaign events or the candidate's barely truthful rhetoric. The public got a flag-wrapped George Bush blasting away at Michael Dukakis's competence and patriotism.

Granted, Dukakis compounded his problems by running a remarkably ineffectual campaign, rarely punching back at Bush or defining his own positions. But Dukakis's ineptitude does not excuse press complaisance. Journalists' responsibility is to peel back the symbols and gimmicks and report the issues and principles at the heart of choosing a new president. Further, when symbolism is especially contrived—such as a Bush media event at a flag factory—the public should be told what is going on.

Another choice for the press is to deemphasize the trappings of the campaign. Instead of giving the flag factory visit two minutes on the evening news, give it ten seconds and then talk about Bush's record on an issue the media select—the record as the journalists have found it through their own investigation, not as presented gift-wrapped by the candidate's handlers.

Many journalists realized that they'd been suckered in 1988 and changed their ways in 1992. Aside from a few grotesqueries such as the Gennifer Flowers extravaganza, focus remained more on issues. On most days, the daily media event circus per se received less coverage.

In an analysis for *The New Republic* in 1992, Mickey Kaus noted how things had changed. He cited a mid-September campaign visit by Bush to Enid, Oklahoma. Against a properly patriotic backdrop, the President attacked Bill Clinton as being a product of "Oxford in the 1960s" and a fan of "social engineering." Bush added, "From Santa Monica to Cambridge, my opponents are cranking up their models, ready to test them on you."[5]

If the 1992 campaign had been proceeding according to the pattern of 1988, this speech would have led the nightly Bush coverage on the network newscasts. It would have been a plus for Bush—an attack inspiring voter worry about Clinton. But this time, none of the networks used any sound from the Enid appearance—just a few seconds of pictures, then on to other business. That's progress.

But whenever the press-politician balance seems to have been readjusted to the public's benefit, unforeseen circumstances can throw things out of whack. In 1992, the Ross Perot candidacy presented the press with a particularly difficult challenge. How do you cover a candidate who devotes most of his campaign schedule to studio tapings of paid advertising?

Perot shied away from traditional media events, which was fine, but also from most direct contact with voters and reporters. With his enormous wealth, he could use television "infomercials" to define himself and his candidacy however he pleased. Journalists trying to cover him found that many of their Perot stories—whether about issues or the candidate's alleged idiosyncrasies—had to be done without firsthand material from Perot. The candidate screamed that he was being treated unfairly, but the public was the real loser. People were asked to make their voting decisions based on incomplete information.

The Perot approach can be categorized as passive manipulation of news coverage. It lacks the blatant mendacity that permeates much of the campaign road show, but it still is designed to keep reporters off balance and to make news coverage a candidate's tool rather than a voter's aid.

Approaches may change, but efforts to manipulate the news media will always be with us. The best the public can hope for is that reporters will remain aware of this and do their best to counteract it.

THE WATCHDOGS' ROLE

Offering voters whatever they need to cast an informed ballot is part of journalists' role as guardians of the political process. That's a big job, requiring more than watchfulness. It also involves taking affirmative measures to champion interests that politicians might otherwise ignore.

For instance, the homeless, the mentally ill, and members of small ethnic minorities may have legitimate needs, but because they can't grease political wheels with lobbying and large contributions, and because they aren't a force at the polls, issues that matter most to them aren't likely to get much attention. Among these issues are Native Americans' land claims, wheelchair access to public buildings, psychiatric treatment for mentally ill prisoners . . . the list is long, the topics sometimes obscure. News coverage can partly compensate for these groups' lack of size and wealth, pushing their issues onto the campaign agenda. If the press doesn't do this, probably no one will.

Other inclusion decisions for news organizations involve parties or independent candidates that operate outside the mainstream. Some, such as the Libertarian Party, have a support base sufficient to get their presidential candidates on all fifty states' ballots. But intellectual inertia tends to make journalists protectors of the status quo. They treat the Democratic-Republican hegemony as sacrosanct, departing from this only in the rare instances when an attention-grabbing celebrity such as Ross Perot or a major party defector such as George Wallace or John Anderson puts together an independent candidacy.

This underscores press power. As the Libertarians have learned, without the credibility that news coverage provides, they are unlikely to pry many voters away from Democratic and Republican ranks.

Granted, the news media—especially the electronic media—face format constraints that limit the scope of coverage. On an always crowded newscast, some stories about some candidates simply aren't going to get on the air. Even major party politicians discover this during crowded primary campaigns, when "front-runners" are helped to perpetuate that status because journalists give minimal air time and column inches to contenders back in the pack. This makes labeling a candidate a front-runner a self-fulfilling prophecy.

To some degree, this narrowing is unavoidable. But news organizations should realize that it's not just a matter of journalistic housekeeping. The scope of coverage defines the scope of the political universe that voters are most likely to explore. Limiting voters' choices inhibits the political dynamic that fosters structural change.

Ross Perot's ascendance could alter this. If he finds a way to channel his celebrity and resources into building a new party—one that is more than a personal vehicle for him—the news media almost certainly will treat it seriously. But Perot's bank account doesn't by itself make his venture more worthy of attention than any other party—Libertarian, Natural Law, Socialist Worker, and so on. The field is crowded, and the requirements of fairness are hard to define.

Likewise, the list of the journalistic sentinel's responsibilities is virtually endless. Those who work in the news business sometimes forget that they play an essential role in maintaining the political system's balance. The American political process is too important to be entrusted solely to the politicians, but it also is too fragile to sustain batterings induced by a careless, unfair press. Sensationalism, inaccuracies, and bias take a heavy toll.

Also, even the most conscientious journalists must realize that the power they wield is intrinsically fragile. By shining their spotlight on issues and candidates, they can do much to help the public police its own system. But this influence is principally that of moral suasion. Other than having a few legal tools—such as laws requiring open meetings and ensuring access to some government information—journalists rarely force open the door to news. They cannot compel sources to talk or subjects of coverage to cooperate.

Despite the fundamentally adversarial nature of the relationship between politicians and journalists, a certain amount of cooperation is essential, based on shared belief in the overriding importance of *the system*. The water in which both reporters and candidates swim must be kept pure.

WHEN POLITICS AND JOURNALISM MIX—TALES OF TWO PUBLISHERS

Maintaining systemic integrity never has been easy. Crooked politicians and dishonest journalists have risen to prominence in their respective trades. But these constitute small minorities in each profession.

Sometimes journalistic and political paths converge. When this sharing of common ground takes place, difficult ethical questions arise, as the following examples illustrate.

Horace Greeley

Among the 19th-century newspaper giants was Horace Greeley, editor of the *New York Tribune*, which he founded in 1841. When the Civil War began, Greeley was unenthusiastic about Abraham Lincoln's leadership. In his memoirs, published in 1868, Greeley said of Lincoln, "I hold him most inapt for the leadership of a people involved in a desperate, agonizing war."[6] The president, trying to maintain popular support for the war, was so intent on winning Greeley's backing that he agreed to leak advance word about administration policies to the *Tribune*. Having Greeley in his corner, said Lincoln, "will be as helpful to me as an army of 100,000 men."[7]

Greeley's hot- and-cold attitudes about Lincoln were reflected in the *Tribune*'s editorials. That's certainly legitimate journalism. But in 1863, Greeley—who worried that the Union's cause was doomed— privately approached the French government about mediating an end to the war.[8] For all his power and fame as an editor, Greeley was still a private citizen, elected by no one. His overtures to the French carried him beyond the realm of journalism and into the domain of politics.

Trying to keep a foot in each world put Greeley in an untenable position. For one thing, such private diplomacy was of questionable legality. Also, he was making news rather than just reporting it.

After the war, Greeley became increasingly active in politics, now out in the open. He sought the Republican nomination for governor of New York in 1868, ran unsuccessfully for Congress in 1870, and served as a member of the Republican National Committee. In 1872, he bolted from the main-stream Republican party and became a presidential candidate, challenging the Republican incumbent, Ulysses S. Grant.

Greeley was nominated by the ragtag Liberal Republican movement, and his support for amnesty for the South also won him the Democratic nomination. He took a leave of absence from the *Tribune* during the campaign, but he could not erase the prevalent public perception of him as a journalist. Some of his press colleagues savaged him. Thomas Nast, the best-known editorial cartoonist of his day, was particularly vicious, depicting Greeley as having been driven beyond all scruples by his ambition. The *Springfield* (Ill.) *Republican* called his candidacy "a crime in journalism."[9]

Greeley didn't have much chance of defeating Grant. Although he ended up with 44 percent of the popular vote, he didn't carry a single state.

The *Tribune* long had been identified so closely with Greeley that many people's opinion of the *Tribune* was essentially their opinion of Greeley. He issued a postelection pronouncement that the *Tribune* would henceforth function as an independent, nonpartisan publication.[10] But that was a politician's, not a journalist's, claim; the *Tribune* had come to be perceived as a politician's, not a journalist's newspaper.

Greeley's wife had died just a few days before the election, and he never recovered from the combination of personal and electoral loss. He returned to the *Tribune* several days after the election, but his physical and mental health were in ruins. He died a few weeks later.

A principal ethical lesson to be derived from the latter stages of Greeley's career is that editorial partisanship is fine; the public expects it. But participatory partisanship—doing politics instead of just reporting and commenting about it—is very different. The wall between the two needs to be kept in good repair. Once that wall is breached, public trust will spill away.

William Randolph Hearst

Another journalist who made forays into politics was William Randolph Hearst. He was publisher of the *New York Journal* (later renamed the *New York American*), and by the time of his death in 1951, he headed a media empire comprising eighteen newspapers plus other media businesses.

Hearst proceeded on several fronts. Pursuing his own career, he was elected to Congress from New York in 1902 and sought the Democratic presidential nomination in 1904 (coming in a distant second at the convention to nominee Alton B. Parker). He also was an unsuccessful candidate for mayor of New York City and governor of New York. On and off, he dreamed of starting a third party that would champion the cause of "the masses" and propel him into the White House.[11]

Despite his thirst for elective office, Hearst became best known for shamelessly subjecting his newspapers' readers to one-sided propaganda about issues and people. His most famous cause was the Spanish-American War, which some Hearst watchers believe could have been avoided had Hearst not been in a circulation war with fellow New York press lord Joseph Pulitzer, publisher of the *New York World*.[12]

One story—possibly apocryphal—illustrates Hearst's approach. Before the war, he sent famed artist Frederic Remington to Cuba to provide pictures of the goings-on there. Remington found little excitement, so he sent Hearst a telegram: "Everything is quiet. There is no trouble here. There will be no war. I wish to return." Hearst's response: "Please remain. You furnish the pictures and I'll furnish the war."

He was as good as his word. After the explosion of the U.S. battleship *Maine* in Havana harbor in 1898, the *Journal*'s coverage was florid and, according to Hearst biographer W. A. Swanberg, "still stands as the orgasmic acme of ruthless, truthless newspaper jingoism."[13] Despite abject Spanish condolences and much uncertainty about the cause of the explosion, Hearst orchestrated a crescendo of prowar sentiment.

Here is a sampling of the banner headlines from the *Journal*:[14] February 16 (the day after the explosion), "CRUISER MAINE BLOWN UP IN HAVANA HARBOR" (true enough); February 17, "THE CRUISER MAINE WAS SPLIT IN TWO BY AN ENEMY'S SECRET INFERNAL MACHINE"; February 18, "THE WHOLE COUNTRY THRILLS WITH THE WAR FE-

VER"; February 21, "HAVANA POPULACE INSULTS THE MEMORY OF
THE MAINE VICTIMS"; and so on. When Congress approved a declara-
tion of war in April, the *Journal* headline reflected Hearst's pleasure: "NOW
TO AVENGE THE MAINE."

This self-serving zeal continued. For a time, bold type at the top of the
Journal's front page asked readers a revealing question: "HOW DO YOU
LIKE THE JOURNAL'S WAR?"[15]

"The *Journal*'s War" meant Hearst's war. It was a war the public—in-
flamed by some of its newspapers—supported despite the lack of political
or security threats that might have made war necessary. The Spanish
government did all it could to avoid war, and President William McKinley
was notably unenthusiastic about it. But Hearst wanted it, and so he led a
pack of jingoistic journalists and politicians (including soon-to-be Rough
Rider Theodore Roosevelt) in howling for battle.

The war produced plenty of lively reporting and sold lots of newspapers.
That, to Hearst's mind, was justification enough. He clearly thought he was
well within his journalistic rights to act as such an incendiary political force.

The Spanish-American War was a brief and not particularly bloody conflict. American casualties totaled fewer than 400 dead and about 3,700
wounded. Not big numbers, but these men—plus many Spaniards and
Cubans—might have escaped harm had Hearst and his colleagues not felt so
free to use them as pawns. Hearst knew what he was promising when he told
Frederic Remington that he would furnish a war. He understood his power.

Hearst and the *Journal* could have played straight with the sinking of the
Maine, not printing unsubstantiated charges and devoting appropriate
coverage to Spain's conciliatory conduct. Headlines could have been calm
rather than inflammatory. Probably fewer papers would have been sold.
But this would have been responsible journalism. Also, a war might have
been avoided.

Legally, Hearst was within his rights. The First Amendment protects
most untruthful and sensationalistic journalism. But that which is legal is
not always ethical. Conflicts between legal and ethical standards occur
often. The journalist involved must decide how far to stretch press freedom.
In such cases, William Randolph Hearst is not much of a role model.

RAKING MUCK

Exercising political clout is an integral part of journalism. Presumably,
the audience takes seriously at least some of what the news media provide.
The only way for public opinion not to be influenced would be to make
news reports so bland that nobody would care about them. So journalists'
claims of being neutral are disingenuous. Even the daily selection of which
stories to publish and which to exclude is not a neutral act. Choice—unless
based on a flip of a coin—has an intellectual basis.

This exercise of influence is either benign or dangerous, depending on the eye of the beholder. William Randolph Hearst's provocative headlines might be condemned by the same person who applauds similarly loud journalism on behalf of a cause he or she happens to support.

The basic test of shrill or staid journalism should be "Is it true?" Much of the Hearst-directed coverage of the *Maine* explosion didn't meet that standard, and so is an easy target for ethicists. But do similar problems arise when a news story is factually sound while also being blatantly partisan? Is ethical journalism endangered when the line between hard news reporting and editorializing blurs? Or are ethics well served by journalists who ferret out painful truths and deliver them with a passion guaranteed to make the public take notice? Such questions arise when considering the role of the muckrakers.

The first writers to be labeled "muckrakers" were those who provided the drumbeat for the march of Progressive politics during the first years of the twentieth century. Candidates such as Theodore Roosevelt campaigned on promises to bust the corporate trusts and to give more Americans a taste of economic justice, while journalists such as Ida Tarbell and Lincoln Steffens blasted away at targets such as Standard Oil Company and corrupt big city politicians.

These articles—appearing in magazines such as *McClure's* and *Everybody's*—were widely read, and as the public took notice, so did government. Among the laws passed with impetus from the muckrakers were the following:[16]

— Hepburn Act (1906), authorizing tighter regulation of railroads; followed "Railroads on Trial," by Ray Stannard Baker in *McClure's*

— Meat Inspection Act (1906), mandating closer supervision of the meat-packing industry; followed Upton Sinclair's fact-based novel, *The Jungle*

— Pure Food and Drug Act (1906), cracking down on the patent medicine industry; followed Samuel Hopkins Adams's "The Great American Fraud" in *Collier's*.

Solid reporting that informs the public and leads to political reform might seem to be journalism at its best. But some people took exception to the journalists' zeal. Among them was President Theodore Roosevelt, who at first had considered these same reporters to be his allies. By 1906, he was angry with them, and in a famous speech dubbed them "muckrakers," a term he meant to be anything but complimentary:

In Bunyan's *Pilgrim's Progress* you may recall the description of the Man with the Muckrake, the man who could look no way but downward, with a muckrake in his hands; who was offered a celestial crown for his muckrake, but who would neither look up nor regard the crown he was offered, but continued to rake to himself the filth of the floor.

The Man with the Muckrake, continued Roosevelt,

typifies the man who in this life consistently refuses to see aught that is lofty, and fixes his eyes with solemn intentness only on that which is vile and debasing. Now, it is very necessary that we should not flinch from seeing what is vile and debasing. There is filth on the floor, and it must be scraped up with the muckrake; and there are times and places where this service is the most needed of all the services that can be performed. But the man who never does anything else, who never thinks or speaks or writes save of his feats with the muckrake, speedily becomes not a help to society, not an incitement to good, but one of the most potent forces of evil.

Roosevelt went on to caution against making false charges: "The soul of every scoundrel is gladdened whenever an honest man is assailed, or when a scoundrel is untruthfully assailed." He also criticized the tone of some journalism: "Hysterical sensationalism is the very poorest weapon where-with to fight for lasting righteousness."[17]

Presumably to the president's dismay, some of the journalists he was chastising liked his imagery and proudly adopted the label "muckraker."

Semantics aside, Roosevelt's message included some ideas worth re-membering. One of his points is that preoccupation with ferreting out evil can lead to misjudging or ignoring that which is good, thereby producing unbalanced, unfair reporting. Perspective, argued Roosevelt, must be kept sufficiently broad to ensure that not everyone in a particular class—such as politicians or business executives—is presumed to be "vile and debasing."

The muckrakers of Roosevelt's time and their descendants today share a tendency to treat subjects of some stories as guilty until proven innocent. That's not fair, and it often isn't accurate. Similarly, "hysterical sensation-alism" is not effective—especially over the long run—in stimulating re-form. Reasoned argument works better.

Roosevelt's fundamental point is that journalists should occasionally look up from the muck—even though not surrendering their rakes—just to get their bearings and recall that good, as well as evil, exists.

Balance is the key: balancing aggressiveness and thoughtfulness, keep-ing fairness and accuracy paramount. Doing so can sustain muckraking and make it even more effective.

THE SLEEPING WATCHDOG

The relentless investigations of the muckrakers may occasionally have taken wrong turns, but a more common journalistic failing has been pas-sivity—turning a blind eye to wrongdoing, or being excessively cautious, so as not to offend the powers that be.

Such behavior by journalists has ebbed and flowed. For instance, until recent years, politicians' drunkenness and adultery were generally ignored by reporters (more about this in Chapter 3). Maybe that's just respecting officeholders' privacy; maybe it's depriving news consumers of information they need to know.

One example of the fuzzy distinction between the two: During the 1944 presidential campaign, anyone who spent time around Franklin Roosevelt knew that he was a very sick man, and a good chance existed that he would not live out his fourth term if reelected. Most reporters did not aggressively question the president or his doctors about this, and didn't raise the issue in their stories.

Of course, this was in the midst of World War II, and so keeping the president's fragile health a secret may be said to have been a wise national security decision. But that's letting the press off too easily. This was part of a pattern of complaisance—of never showing the polio-stricken president's leg braces in photographs, of letting him keep his comments off the record whenever he chose, and of being generally protective and supportive. Such treatment is appropriate coming from the politician's aides, but not from journalists.

This is the essence of being "on the team." That phrase became famous during the Vietnam War when an admiral was unhappy with reporter Malcolm Browne, whose tough reporting was dampening enthusiasm for the war. The admiral asked Browne, "Why don't you get on the team?"

While pondering this, long-time White House correspondent James Deakin asked a counterquestion: "If the journalists are on the team, who will report the game?"[18]

Although government officials may be quick to claim that joining the team will be in the nation's best interests, things don't always work out that way. A good example can be seen in news coverage of preparations for the American-backed invasion of Cuba in 1961.

A *New York Times* reporter had gathered convincing information that anti-Castro Cubans, with the blessing of the Kennedy administration, were preparing to invade their homeland. Concerned about sending too explicit a signal to Castro and others about the invasion, *Times* editors watered down the story (by, for example, removing the word "imminent" in describing the invasion) and using a relatively innocuous headline. President Kennedy, nevertheless, reportedly was furious about the disclosure: "Castro doesn't need agents over here. All he has to do is read our papers."[19]

The story was accurate, and the invasion took place. It was a total disaster. The invading force never got beyond its landing site at the Bay of Pigs, and Castro scored a resounding triumph.

Soon thereafter, President Kennedy in a speech urged journalists to ask themselves if their stories are "in the interest of national security." But several weeks later, Kennedy told *Times* managing editor Turner Catledge, "Maybe if you had printed more about the operation you would have saved us from a colossal mistake."[20]

The *Times* had gotten on the team. But that's not where it should have been. If the paper had delivered the news and not pulled its punches, perhaps Kennedy would have halted the invasion. And even if he hadn't, at least the public would have known about the government's foolhardy policy.

News professionals' worrying about being on the team is a symptom of an identity crisis. It reflects a belief that they must choose between journalism and patriotism. That distinction rarely exists. There's nothing unpatriotic about delivering accurate, complete information to the public. The government can take care of itself. It won't crumble just because the public knows what it's doing.

Overcautious journalism occurs often, and not just when the government is in the midst of a crisis. Reporters sometimes become mere recipients rather than true gatherers of the news.That may seem a fine line, but it's an important distinction.

For example, in its early days, television news—hamstrung by demands of its still-awkward technology—often covered that which was easiest to cover. According to media critic Barbara Matusow, "the predictable or staged event, filmed mainly in New York or Washington, became a staple of early TV news."[21]

Of course, early television also featured the courageous, probing reporting of Edward R. Murrow and other pioneers of the genre. And by no means has television ever been alone in being guilty of lazy reporting. But some of the sharpest criticism has been directed at TV news.

Michael Arlen, television writer for *The New Yorker*, provided a demanding voice in the debate about the adequacy of coverage of the Vietnam War. In one 1966 essay, he criticized NBC's reporting from a Manila summit meeting of the United States and its Pacific allies:

It's hard to avoid the feeling that NBC either isn't telling all it knows or else doesn't know very much. . . . I wonder if NBC's television-news people really understand the degree of complicity with official government policy that they achieve by presenting government statements at face value and then simply not asking the questions that intelligent men are bound to be concerned about.[22]

Presumably in this case, NBC was not making a conscious effort to be a mouthpiece for Lyndon Johnson's administration. But sloppy, unenterprising reporting leads to a de facto transformation of the news product from journalism to propaganda.

The ethical responsibility is clear: once again, allegiance must be to the news consumer, not the news source. In this instance, according to Arlen, NBC's loyalties became muddled.

THE NEW ACTIVISM

Not long after Arlen wrote that essay, the news business entered a period of rapid maturing and revived activism. The Vietnam War and the Watergate scandal were the principal catalysts.

Journalists became aware of persistent misrepresentation by the government, first about the status of the war and then about the extent of White House involvement in a criminal conspiracy. As the government became increasingly estranged from the public, some news organizations began taking their role as the public's surrogate more seriously. Coverage of the war became more comprehensive and critical, and reporting about Watergate helped Americans scrutinize the Nixon presidency.

The political system—as nebulous as it often seems—requires loyal maintenance. This is not outside the journalist's responsibility. The campaign of the moment—whether a race for president or for justice of the peace—can seem to be of cosmic consequence. But it rarely is. Despite the tendency to become caught up in the day-to-day whirl, reporters must maintain a long view, recognizing that most events looming so large today are actually just tiny chips in a grand mosaic.

In practice, this translates into playing a constructively adversarial role, not trashing candidates without cause and not letting cynicism—of which there is plenty among journalists—distort coverage.

Many voters are skeptical about the viability of the political process. That's healthy if not carried too far. It becomes debilitating, however, if hopelessness prevails and voting is abandoned as being pointless. Journalists should realize that they have considerable influence on the public's attitudes about this process.

WHO'S IN CHARGE?

To a considerable extent, campaign coverage is like a tug-of-war. Journalists want good stories; politicians want good stories. "Good," however, will be defined in different ways. From the reporter's standpoint, a good story is interesting and informative. For the politician, a good story is one that helps him or her win votes.

Throughout a campaign, politicians will try to pull reporting toward their definition of "good," while journalists try to haul it in the other direction.

This is far more than a childish game. Both sides know the stakes involved. News coverage does affect voting behavior. It isn't wholly determinative of how people vote, but it is influential.

Sometimes this influence is subtle; sometimes it's as subtle as being slammed by a sledgehammer. A case in point: During the tight 1976 presidential race between Gerald Ford and Jimmy Carter, Ford announced that he would veto legislation authorizing a financial bailout of New York City. The *New York Daily News* ran this strident headline: "FORD TO CITY: DROP DEAD." Coming just a few days before the election, that may have tilted some New York voters toward Carter.[23] The Democratic challenger won the state by less than 300,000 votes out of more than 6 million cast. Had New York's forty-one electoral votes gone to the Republicans, Ford would have remained in the White House for another four years.

That example relies on hypothetical history, and so is far from conclusive. But it offers some idea of the impact news coverage can have. It also underscores the significance of ethical or unethical behavior. President Ford had clearly explained why he didn't want to set a bailout precedent for local governments and why he wanted New York to do more to solve its own problems.[24] He never told New York to "drop dead." The inflammatory headline may have been typical of the *News*'s style, and so its message may have been discounted by readers, but that doesn't make it ethical.

During most campaigns, the news media influence voters less through extraordinary, screaming-headline stories than through the quiet flow of daily coverage. Here is where a candidate and his or her handlers must prove their mettle. They want voters exposed to their campaign on their terms; they want the news media to be their messengers.

In presidential campaigns, this effort is most visible in the daily schedule of "media events" and "press availabilities." These are carefully designed to present the candidate's image and message in the most favorable light. The media events are often Hollywood-type extravaganzas, featuring bands, balloons, and American flags . . . lots of American flags. Ideally, a cheering throng will be on hand to watch, but that's important only to add energy to the tableau. The real audience will be sitting at home that evening, catching maybe thirty seconds of the festivities while watching a newscast.

All the planning and expense that go into these productions are aimed at that result: a few moments of exposure that will link—in the voter's mind—the candidate to the patriotic grandeur and campaign momentum depicted on the screen. The news media provide free delivery of this carefully crafted package.

That's the campaign's visual content. Intellectual content is supplied through press availabilities. In carefully run campaigns, that's something of a misnomer, because the candidate is available only on his or her terms. The message of the day is delivered by the candidate, and reporters' questions are answered tersely, if at all.

By limiting access, campaign managers can control what the press corps reports. Reporters need to produce stories; they have to make do with what they can get. Most of them would prefer, of course, to see a full-blown daily news conference so they could decide on the topics for discussion and force the candidate to conform to their agenda. But the candidate's handlers know how dangerous that can be. Based on their polling and expertise, they have decided how they want to woo voters. They don't want reporters to push the campaign in some other direction.

In 1984 and 1988, the Reagan and Bush campaigns were enormously successful in shaping each day's coverage to meet their needs. They decided what issues they wanted to stress; designed their schedule, events, and press availabilities accordingly; and stuck to their plan. On the other hand, their opponents, Walter Mondale and Michael Dukakis, never seemed to understand how the media game was played.

In this contest for control, the politicians may seem to have more muscle. But reporters aren't without their own strength. Their enterprise need not be limited by the politicians' maneuvers. First, they must decide what the public needs to know. Then they should provide it. If the candidate is uncooperative, they can search elsewhere.

A big part of this is screening politician-originated events and material. Not everything the candidate does or says must be reported to the public. If a media event is meaningless—contributing nothing to the information base voters need—journalists can simply ignore it. Relying on the fundamental test of newsworthiness could eliminate much of the dross from campaign reporting.

Most politicians would conform, however grudgingly, to tougher standards (at least until they find some way to circumvent them, too). They always need coverage, so they will have to compromise to meet journalistic assertiveness. When faced with the choice of providing substance or not being covered, most will choose the former.

TARGETING THE PRESS

In this high-stakes game, the politicians have another tactic at their disposal—press bashing. Richard Nixon's vice president, Spiro Agnew, found his niche in that administration when he delivered several speeches chastising journalists. His speeches found a large, appreciative audience among the "silent majority" at which much Nixonian politicking was targeted.

Among Agnew's points were these:

As with other American institutions, perhaps it is time that the networks were made more responsive to the views of the nation and more responsible to the people they serve.[25]

And in the networks' endless pursuit of controversy, we should ask what is the end value—to enlighten or to profit? What is the end result—to inform or to confuse?[26]

I do not seek to intimidate the press, the networks or anyone else from speaking out. But the time for blind acceptance of their opinions is past. And the time for naive belief in their neutrality is gone.[27]

The strategy behind such remarks was simple: the best way to counteract hostile news coverage is to destroy the credibility of those providing that coverage. Agnew painted the portrait of a mean-spirited, biased press corps dedicated to undermining the Nixon administration. To the delight of the president, Agnew clearly rattled news executives, eliciting a spate of defensive replies.

Most press bashing is not as overt as Agnew's crusade was, but the basic purpose remains the same. Get the public angry about alleged press unfairness and hope this forces aggressive reporters to back off.

An example of this was the 1988 counterattack by Republican vice presidential nominee Dan Quayle against a press corps that had been pounding him ever since George Bush had selected him as his running mate. Following the Bush announcement, Quayle endured several days of being quizzed about purported character flaws—principally his Vietnam-era service in the National Guard.

After the Republican National Convention concluded in New Orleans, Quayle traveled to Huntington, Indiana, to speak to a friendly, home-state crowd. Immediately following the speech, Quayle took questions from reporters, but he did so over a public address system that let his 5,000 supporters present hear the questions and answers. As the tough questioning proceeded, the pro-Quayle crowd grew more hostile, loudly booing the reporters. The national audience, watching excerpts of this on the nightly news, saw an all-American, flag-draped courthouse square where the besieged hometown boy was fending off a journalistic feeding frenzy.[28]

This turned out to be something of a triumph for Quayle, the first good outing he'd had since the press barrage had begun a few days before. Successfully portraying himself as press victim, Quayle won sympathy from many who hadn't made up their minds about his qualifications, but who knew they didn't like seeing reporters ganging up on anyone.

That kind of reaction is something reporters shouldn't forget. It underscores the fragility of the press's status as sentinel, keeping watch over the political battle lines, warning the public about transgressions by campaigners. To fulfill this responsibility, journalists must enjoy the trust of their readers, listeners, and viewers. Without public faith in their mission, news organizations will find themselves in the untenable position of being uncredible messengers who usually bring only bad news.

If that happens, the messages will increasingly be disregarded, and political journalism will cease to matter to those it is supposed to serve.

Chapter Two

Journalists' Competence

Being competent isn't just a good idea; it's an ethical responsibility. To put it another way, a journalist has an ethical obligation not to be an idiot.

Competence requires knowledge. In political journalism, that means understanding the issues and mechanics of campaigns. Learning about all this requires enormous amounts of time and effort, but there's no way to avoid it. Taking shortcuts—skipping the background research, not challenging the campaign consultant's claims—will produce weak journalism. The reporter's career might flourish on the basis of flashy, superficial coverage. Sometimes show biz values take precedence over "pure journalism" in the news business. But whenever this happens, the public is cheated.

FAIRNESS: REALITY AND ILLUSION

Fairness and competence are inextricably linked. Journalists aren't doing their jobs properly if their coverage is constricted by premeditated bias or even inadvertent lack of evenhandedness. Intent doesn't matter. The news consumer receives damaged goods if reporting isn't fair.

"You reporters are all biased" is probably the most frequently heard complaint about political journalism. Some news professionals dismiss such charges as uninformed whining. To a certain extent, that may be true. Existence of bias often depends on the eye of the beholder. Any coverage that is short of adoration of a favorite candidate or cause may be seen by partisans as a scurrilous attack.

In politics, such complaints come with the territory, creating "them-versus-us" bitterness. During the 1992 campaign, George Bush cited as his favorite bumper sticker message "Annoy the Media—Re-elect Bush."

Partisanship sharpens emotions. But that's okay. If everyone is happy with campaign coverage, it's too bland; reporters must not be doing their jobs correctly.

Despite this, allegations about bias should be treated seriously. If—judged objectively—they are true, coverage is flawed and more attention should be paid to fairness. A number of factors should be considered when evaluating such charges.

First, coverage as a whole rather than a single story should be analyzed. For instance, in the course of the 1992 presidential campaign, major news organizations carried hundreds of stories about the candidates. On any given day, the lead story about George Bush may have seemed more positive than the coverage of Bill Clinton.

An example: During the final week of the campaign, many stories about Bush focused on his "miracle comeback" attempt, while stories about Clinton tended to emphasize his slippage in the opinion polls. Clinton backers saw this coverage as dangerously biased, fueling Bush's efforts while wiping out Clinton's momentum.

But many Bush supporters argue that overall campaign coverage was slanted the other way, pumping up the Clinton candidacy and battering Bush. Press cheerleading that accompanied Clinton's postconvention bus tours offered plenty of evidence supporting that claim.

So both candidates can claim to have been beneficiaries and victims of coverage. Journalists should be evenhanded day in and day out, but candidates—like everyone else—have their good days and their bad days, and coverage will reflect this. In evaluating the 1992 race—or any other campaign—the whole picture should be analyzed. Is the reporting balanced over the long term?

This is a much-examined topic, but many studies allow academic fancy or arithmetical gymnastics to push aside common sense. For instance, research by some intensely serious organizations found that in television network reports about the 1992 presidential campaign, Bush most often was portrayed negatively.[1] These studies—at least as they were summarized for the public—downplayed some important factors:

— Press coverage's long-standing antiestablishment tone. If Bush was dumped on, it was in many cases because he was the incumbent, not because he was the Republican, and not because of press favoritism toward Clinton. In 1980—the last time a Democratic incumbent ran—Jimmy Carter was similarly battered.

— The tendency of negative stories to appear about badly run campaigns, which Bush's undoubtedly was. The same thing happened to Democrat Michael Dukakis in 1988, when his poorly managed campaign became a magnet for critical reporting.

— The greater importance of stories close to Election Day. This is when more positive, "comeback" stories about Bush appeared (but so did new reports about Iran-Contra indictments). When measuring coverage's impact on voters, more weight should be given to stories appearing late in the campaign, when many people are making up their minds about how to vote.

— The decreased significance of traditional news coverage because of the unprecedented access of candidates to "new news" talk shows outside mainstream journalism. Bush and his challengers could dodge hostile journalists and still reach the public (more about this later in this chapter).

All these hard-to-measure factors presumably influenced voters, some more than others.

Another aspect of the fairness issue that is often overlooked occurs when journalists sacrifice accuracy for the sake of fairness, or at least for the sake of *appearing* fair.

This well-intentioned clumsiness could be seen during the 1992 Republican National Convention. Many journalists covering the event knew that the party may have been embarking on a suicidal course when it allowed its convention to be dominated by venomous far-right-wing rhetoric. Comments by national party chair Rich Bond, Patrick Buchanan, Marilyn Quayle, and others may have appealed to the ultraconservative faithful among the convention delegates, but were certain to turn off many of those watching the show on television. In the battle for the crucial "moderate middle" of the electorate, the Republicans committed a major tactical blunder. (For example, Bond—contrasting his party with the Democrats— said, "We are America; these other people are not America.")

Despite journalists' recognizing this, most hard news stories and even analyses at the time refrained from pointing out the full extent of the Republicans' folly. The reason for this reticence: fear that the public would see tough critiques as unfair and proof of anti-Republican bias. So, in the pursuit of "fairness," some journalists pulled their punches, kept their reports bland, and waited until later in the campaign—when the Bush campaign was well on its way to defeat—to point out how damaging the convention had been.

Proceeding so gingerly frequently conflicts with objective reporting, but journalists' sensitivity is understandable. Individually and collectively they are constantly charged with trying to rig the game in which they are the umpires. Some go to considerable lengths to divorce themselves from any personal interest in an election's outcome.

Leonard Downie, Jr., executive editor of the *Washington Post*, decided how he would try to protect his objectivity:

I no longer exercise my right to vote. As the final decision-maker on news coverage in *The Post*, I refuse to decide, even privately, which candidate would be the best president or member of the city council or what position I should take on an issue like abortion or setting taxes. I want my mind to remain open to all sides and possibilities.[2]

Downie notes that this is his own choice, and it is not imposed on those who work for him. Surrendering the vote—especially in a country where voter participation is miserable—is a big step. A small minority of journalists go this far in their efforts to be perceived as being objective. A far larger number worry less about public perceptions and look at maintaining their objectivity as a matter of self-enforced intellectual discipline.

Political abstinence has its detractors. Columnist Michael Kinsley writes:

Some media critics, and some journalists themselves, think that the press ought to function as a sort of sacred priesthood of political celibates, purged of the ideological longings that inflame ordinary folks. . . . [But] journalists, by definition, are inquisitive people with an interest in public affairs. To expect them to form no conclusions about the people and policies they report on is absurd.[3]

Sometimes journalists feel particularly beleaguered about all this because many news consumers don't take note of the difference between reporters who deliver hard news and columnists or analysts who deliver opinion. In the news business, the basic rule is to keep the distinction clear by relying on truth in packaging—labeling opinion as such and keeping clear separation between it and the regular news product.

In the print media, this isn't difficult. The editorial and op ed pages are obviously bastions of opinion, and presumably most readers recognize them as such. Elsewhere in a newspaper or magazine, labels of "analysis," "commentary," "essay," or the like can be used. In the electronic media, labeling also isn't difficult. A tag identifying an opinion report can be superimposed on the television screen, and radio listeners can be told before and after an opinion piece what they're getting.

This labeling or other segregation is extremely important. When walls between news and opinion crumble, charges of bias increase and are more likely to be correct. Some news organizations have gotten sloppy about this. For example, several weekly news magazines do a poor job of keeping sometimes snide "interpretation" out of what appear to be straight news stories.

Of course, people—not robots—decide what elements to include in a news story and what stories to publish. Those decisions are influenced by the journalist's background, experience, and values. This is unavoidable, but as long as it is recognized by the decision maker, this very human trait can enrich rather than distort the news.

The more determinedly fairness is pursued, the more complex the task becomes. Convincing the public of journalistic fairness is a perpetually elusive goal, dependent as it is on the perceptions of disparate audiences. Nevertheless, it is a goal that must not be abandoned. Both reality and perception are important.

UNDERSTANDING ISSUES

Increasing coverage of issues is probably the most frequently cited sign of progress in the evolution of political journalism. But progress doesn't come easily. Reporters find that covering issues properly requires lots of work.

A principal ethical component of issues reporting is analyzing candidates' positions and challenging their assertions. That means checking statistics and seeking solid evidence and theories that reinforce or run contrary to the candidates' claims. This often is difficult, because politicians' statements tend to be as much opinion as fact.

For example, in 1992, when Bill Clinton, George Bush, and Ross Perot offered their plans for deficit reduction, no one could really know if their schemes would be effective. Of course, the politicians were quick to trash each other's plans. Also, plenty of economists could be found who agreed with one or several of the candidates' views, and others were available who thought some or all of the proposals were worthless.

Despite such predictable cloudiness, news organizations should plunge ahead and independently analyze whatever the candidates offer. Reporters can do their own work or rely on selected experts in the field. For instance, many local news organizations rely on professors from a hometown university to provide an academic perspective. These analysts might be interviewed from time to time, or they might be hired as consultants. Whichever approach is used, journalists should try to tap into diverse reservoirs of expertise.

If this isn't done, politicians may try to get away with intellectual murder. Sometimes campaigns generate amazing stuff, based more on fiction than fact, hoping gullible voters will embrace whatever appears to be the most painless way of dealing with complex problems. For example, a gubernatorial candidate might promise to lower automobile insurance rates if elected. The press should tell the public if the governor really has the power to do that, and what the likelihood is of its happening. The average voter doesn't have the wherewithal to check out every issues position, so journalists must be their surrogate researchers.

Voters also can make better sense of the campaign if reporters do their issues stories in ways that can be understood without having a Ph.D.

Suppose, for instance, that the issue at hand is a candidate's proposal for retraining former defense industry workers. Economists and labor experts could be interviewed at length about theoretical merits or flaws of the plan. Most news consumers may be more numbed than enlightened by their pontificating. The reporter could also find some people who would be directly affected if the plan were implemented—for example, laid-off aerospace workers—and interview them about how they and their families would be helped or hurt. This, coupled with experts' analyses, might help the journalists' audience make truly informed judgments about the candidate's idea.

Journalists must be prepared to use these innovative, expandable methods. No reporter can be expected to possess enough expertise to do comprehensive stories about every issue that arises during a campaign. The ethical imperative of being knowledgeable still holds, but it includes supplementing personal knowledge with insight from other sources and bolstering coverage with varied approaches to stories.

Failure to do this can result not only in inadequately explaining topics but even in missing issues altogether. A recent example of this is the belated and incomplete coverage of America's savings-and-loan (S&L) bailout fiasco.

As Howard Kurtz detailed in an article for the *Washington Post Magazine*: "Most reporters simply did not grasp the magnitude of the mess on their hands. The evidence was hidden in plain view." Journalists, says Kurtz, were too cautious in approaching this story.

We were trapped by the conventions of objective journalism, the insistence on quoting experts, when what was needed was some old-fashioned crusading. Conditioned by decades of restraint not to cause panic among depositors, we were afraid to shout fire in a crowded theater. The problem was, the theater was burning down while we quibbled about the intricacies of the fire code.[4]

One of a reporter's most valuable traits is his or her skepticism of official pronouncements. But in the S&L case, most reporters failed to challenge the optimistic prognoses being offered by politicians, who in many instances were mainly trying to dodge blame for the scandal.

This passivity was partly a product of caution and partly of failing to understand the complexities of a multifaceted mess. Texas Congressman Henry Gonzalez was one of the few people in Washington sounding the alarm, but no one was listening. At one point, Gonzalez held a news conference to criticize the unrealistically low estimates of bailout costs. But, said Gonzalez, "Nobody paid any attention. . . . Hardly anyone came. I was embarrassed."[5]

Gonzalez realized that despite his presumed clout as a member of the House Banking Committee, his real power depended on news media power. He couldn't get the public's or other politicians' attention without press coverage.

Intensive news coverage might have brought the crisis to a head sooner, saving taxpayers billions of dollars in mushrooming bailout costs. The S&L story is a good example of what can happen if journalists don't work hard enough or think carefully enough. This was a costly ethical lapse.

UNDERSTANDING POLITICS

Figuring out complex issues may seem daunting, but so is under-standing the complexities of pure politics. Campaign coverage never re-mains wholly on the high plane of policy. Reporters must also be well versed in the intricacies of vote-getting.

Many journalists enjoy this, believing that covering issues is work, while covering politics is fun. That may be true, but plenty of pitfalls await on the apparently more pleasurable path. Many of these dangers are discussed in detail in Chapter 4. For now, reporters' competence and the general style and content of coverage are the topics.

Since the 1960s, reporters have increasingly offered their audiences an insider's view of how campaigns work. Rather than simply reporting, "On October 10, Candidate X spoke to labor leaders in New York and endorsed an increase in the minimum wage," the new-style political journalism would provide this coverage: "By October 10, Candidate X's polling was showing slippage in backing from blue-collar voters. Poll-ster Y met with campaign manager Z and recommended immediate action to counteract this loss of crucial support. So a meeting was arranged with labor leaders where X could unveil his plan for increasing the minimum wage. The candidate's remarks were recorded by his media consultant's film crew and were made the centerpiece of a thirty-second TV spot that was aired frequently in cities with substantial union membership."

That kind of reporting is the descendant of the work of one of America's most influential political journalists, Theodore H. White. In his bestselling and Pulitzer Prize-winning book, *The Making of the President 1960*, White offered a view from inside the presidential campaigns, explaining the why and how of decision making, and thus of president making. He saw the campaign as a glorious drama in which the candidate-protagonists pos-sessed heroic strengths and classic flaws.

Of his approach, White wrote that he believed there might "be some permanent value in the effort of a contemporary reporter to catch the mood and the strains, the weariness, the elation and uncertainties of the men who sought to lead America in the decade of the sixties. For, to me, the central fact of politics has always been the quality of leadership under the pressure of great forces."[6]

The 1960 book was a commercial and critical success, and White wrote *Making of the President* volumes about the 1964, 1968, and 1972 campaigns, plus a summary book looking at all the campaigns from 1960 through 1980. More important, he inspired the next generation of political journalists to examine campaigns not just as a series of static events but as a complex story, rich in characters and plot.

The insider's perspective became an integral element of campaign cov-erage. In books such as Joe McGinniss's *The Selling of the President 1968* (about Richard Nixon's manipulative media campaign) and Tim Crouse's *The Boys on the Bus* (about news coverage of the 1972 race), and in daily journalism, the "Teddy White syndrome" has influenced much political reporting. (The esteem in which White was held by his colleagues is exemplified by the dedication of *Behind the Front Page*, by the *Washington Post*'s David Broder: "In memory of Theodore H. White, who took political reporting to a new level and generously taught many of us how we might do our own jobs a bit better.")

For the most part, the White approach has been a plus, enhancing the public's perspective of what's going on in campaigns. The more the voter knows, the less susceptible he or she is to being conned.

One caveat: journalists should be careful not to rely too heavily on information that is so "inside" that its import is lost on the average news consumer. Many reporters can be classified as political junkies; they need their daily fix of campaign gossip and speculation. Some members of their audience also fall into this category, and appreciate nuances of political gamesmanship. But this is a relatively small group.

For news organizations with a mass audience, the ethical mandate in this matter is to avoid neglecting information needs of the many while catering to interests of the few.

When such slips occur, they usually aren't because of any evil intent; reporters sometimes become so used to the rarefied atmosphere of campaigning that they forget about the "real" world. News isn't helpful if it strikes its consumers as being irrelevant. Coverage of issues that affect the voter's household—such as prospects for a personal income tax increase or improved access to health care—will be seen by many as far more important and interesting than will a report about how the candidate's pollster has devised a new method for surveying undecided voters.

These kinds of stories need not be mutually exclusive. The Teddy White approach can be woven into general coverage and be the basis for supplemental analysis stories. With a bit of planning, diverse interests of diverse audiences can be satisfied.

A related responsibility for the reporter is to recognize, and to avoid being victimized by, the unending con game politicians run as they try to manipulate coverage. Campaign managers and other staff members play on journalists' thirst for inside and technical information. For example, a manager may tell a reporter: "We have the most efficient telephone bank operation of any governor's campaign in this state's history. In this week before the election, we're calling 400 voters every day!" Ideally, from the politician's standpoint, the reporter will then produce a news item describing the candidate's "well-oiled campaign machinery," always useful in convincing voters of a candidate's competence.

But the journalist should be able to judge independently whether a telephone bank making 400 calls a day is really so efficient. Actually, in most states, that number would be exceptionally low, and perhaps be evidence that the campaign is poorly organized.

Reporters should put a politician's claim in context before evaluating it. That requires extensive background knowledge about previous campaigns and the techniques of vote getting. Also—as with issues coverage—outside experts might be called on for their analysis.

As gatekeeper governing the flow of news to the public, the journalist should not let a politician's self-serving propaganda reach voters unless accompanied by substantiation. In this hypothetical example, if the phone bank's operation is judged newsworthy, the journalist should relay to the news consumer not only the campaign's claim about its prowess but also the information needed to judge the accuracy of that claim.

Issues might seem to be more important than pure politics, and therefore to deserve the bulk of coverage. But just as voters need to know about a candidate's positions on tax and defense policies, so, too, they should be informed about the competence and fairness of that candidate's campaign. Issues and political conduct rarely can be wholly divorced; the candidate who is dishonest in campaigning may eventually betray even the noblest-sounding policy promises.

So the political journalist who wants to provide truly comprehensive coverage must possess sufficiently sophisticated understanding of politics to be able to report as thoroughly about campaigning as about governing.

JOURNALISTS' SKILLS

The more you think about the scope of journalists' responsibilities, the more you realize how much they need to know to do their job comprehensively and accurately. In political journalism, four fundamental topics require particular attention: campaign histories, new technologies, changing rules of the game, and coverage decisions.

Campaign Histories

Politics is a continuum. Campaign planners rarely do anything truly revolutionary; they usually just fine-tune their predecessors' strategies and tactics, learning from past mistakes and successes. So, to understand what campaigners are doing and what their chances of success are, a smart journalist will develop an encyclopedic knowledge of elections past. For instance, televised presidential debates date back to 1960, and journalists appraising the impact of a current debate should be able to inform their judgments with historical perspective.

Aside from the nuts and bolts of campaigning, this background also helps issues positions make more sense. In 1992, for example, Bill Clinton's support of the death penalty protected him against charges from Republicans that he was "soft on crime," a perception that had done considerable damage to nominee Michael Dukakis four years before. This had been a nagging problem for Democratic candidates. A good reporter would know about Dukakis's vulnerability on this issue and be able to draw the contrast between the two candidates.

Mastering these topics is not necessarily a function of longevity. In fact, sometimes the correspondent who says, "I remember how it was when I covered Truman versus Dewey," remembers it wrong. Experience on the campaign trail helps, but well-organized research may be even more valuable.

New Technologies

Politics—especially on the national level—is increasingly dependent on computers, satellites, and other sophisticated tools. Journalists, even if not scientifically inclined, must know something about this if they are to understand how up-to-date campaigns are run.

Computer programs sort through voter lists and correlate them with census data, identifying not only those who go to the polls most frequently but also voters' race, income level, and (in some states) party affiliation. Given the wide variety of computerized lists now available for purchase, voter targeting has become very precise.

Similarly, telephone solicitation of voters is sometimes now a wholly mechanical, computer-based operation. Mailings to voters are personalized; computers may insert the voter's name several times in the candidate's request for votes or funds. Also, campaigners use satellites to feed videotaped news releases or to offer candidates for "exclusive" long-distance interviews.

Most of these methods are perfectly legitimate, even though they create the illusion that candidates are in closer touch with the voter than they really are. But sometimes what the candidate proclaims to be offering isn't what the voter really gets. For instance, Ross Perot in 1992 advertised a toll-free telephone number that he urged people to call to tell him whether he should reenter the presidential race. He didn't initially say that each call received would be automatically tabulated as a "Yes" vote for his candidacy. Callers who wanted Perot to stay out of the contest had to make their opinion known some other way.

This kind of gimmickry is on the rise. The more innovative such gambits become, the greater the potential for manipulation of voters. If a politician is sophisticated enough to use these techniques, a journalist should know enough to tell the public how they work.

Changing Rules of the Game

The rules governing politics are rarely static. In some areas, such as campaign finance, changes are frequent and complex. For the news consumer observing a campaign, the line between legal and illegal money raising and spending can become blurred.

Similarly complicated are nominating procedures, which vary state by state and party by party. During each presidential year, for instance, news consumers puzzle over the intricacies of the Iowa caucuses, which are the first formal steps in selecting the delegates who eventually will pick the presidential nominee. Rarely does a campaign go by without some controversy about filing deadlines, slate composition, or other such baffling matters.

The journalist's responsibility is to watch all this carefully and report about it knowledgeably. The latter requires perpetual immersion in the arcane procedural maneuverings that many politicians seem to love. In the cosmic scheme of things, how a handful of Iowa delegates gets picked may seem inconsequential, but those news consumers who want to know about it deserve accurate and informative reporting.

As with learning about campaign histories and political technology, mastering the rules of the game demands careful research. That's not much fun; it's a far cry from the joyously frantic pilgrimage along the campaign trail. Nevertheless, it needs doing.

Coverage Decisions

Perhaps the greatest power held by political journalists is their authority to decide what to cover and what to ignore.

This gatekeeper role—deciding what news gets to the public—should be taken seriously. Reporting those news items that turn out to be important sometimes is a matter of luck, but most often it's a product of informed analysis. In the mid-1980s, for example, journalists had to evaluate the significance of Byzantine wheelings and dealings that became known as the Iran-Contra scandal. That took research, investigation, and a thoughtful understanding of the Constitution. Likewise, decisions about how intensively to cover a particular candidate within a large field should be based on knowledge—not guesswork—about the campaign's viability.

On the other side of the coin, journalists must know when to block false information from reaching the public. For example, if a serious charge is leveled at a public figure by a political opponent, should it be reported automatically? Some might say it's news and the public has a right to know about it. But suppose it's not true. Reporting the charge will do damage that might not be repaired even if the correct story eventually comes to light (more about this later in this chapter). Whenever possible, hard facts, not gossip-based intuition, should be the basis of deciding whether to run or kill (or at least delay) the original story.

The many issues outlined here illustrate how difficult intellectually responsible reporting can be. Given journalists' power and the protection the Constitution affords them, the temptation always exists to shoot from the hip, print everything, and let subjects of coverage and news consumers fend for themselves.

But few news organizations endorse such an approach. They take responsibility for their news product, and most realize that this responsibility can be discharged ethically only by knowledgeable journalists.

POLITICIANS' END RUNS

No matter how honestly journalists try to do their jobs, politicians will never wholly trust the news media. Nor will they ever rely exclusively on news organizations' decisions about what to report and how to report it. So politicians look for ways to manipulate news outlets or find other channels for conveying their messages.

A common alternative is advertising. With virtually total control over content, the politician can shape the message however he or she desires. This approach, however, is expensive. Rare is the candidate who can afford enough advertising to match the amount of exposure news coverage provides. Also, most voters are smart enough to know that ads are one-sided, so their influence is limited.

Politicians want the best of two worlds: the credibility inherent in news coverage while avoiding journalists' scrutiny. In 1992, looking to have it both ways, all three major presidential candidates became enamored of "new news."

This genre has been around for a long time. Examples are plentiful, nationally and locally: the talk show presided over by a sometimes minimally informed (and sometimes minimally intelligent) host or hostess; the forum for viewers or listeners to call in with questions—some germane, some irrelevant—for the program's guest.

Nothing is intrinsically wrong with this direct contact between candidate and public. In fact, callers sometimes ignore the political trivia that journalists think so important and cut to the heart of issues, such as by asking, "How will voting for you help me get a job?"

Problems, however, arise in two ways. First, skillful candidates usually can sidestep difficult queries form inexperienced questioners. Also, the glorified disk jockey presiding over these programs rarely asks tough follow-up questions.

These shows become forums for self-advertising, with the politicians able to control much of the tone and content. They can do much to boost the candidate's image but little to help the audience make informed voting decisions.

The biggest problem that arose in 1992 was the tendency of candidates— especially Ross Perot—to use talk shows as a substitute for, rather than a supplement to, true news programs. Perot, for instance, made "The Larry

King Show" his second home while doing his best to avoid programs such as "This Week with David Brinkley" and "Meet the Press." From Perot's standpoint, this was a smart move, because King was more worshipful than inquisitorial. Dealing with King (or Phil Donahue or Arsenio Hall) certainly seemed preferable to fending off barbs from the likes of Sam Donaldson. Relying on these programs plus massive amounts of paid advertising, Perot was able to minimize his dependence on standard news vehicles.

Some harsh criticism was directed at this style of campaigning. Jonathan Yardley of the *Washington Post* noted the difference between the televised debates—admittedly far from flawless—and the talk shows:

The debates may well prove to be as shallow and frivolous as everything else this campaign has unearthed, but their basic purpose is serious; whatever else they may be, the debates are not intended as entertainment, as *show*. But the vast majority of the other television and radio programs to which the candidates are scurrying with such unseemly eagerness are just that: trivial amusements that reduce the candidates to the lowest common Hollywood denominator.[7]

Journalists must decide how to handle the talk-show candidacy. Blasting Perot for this strategy may seem to be just sour grapes. But if journalists take seriously the need for candidates to submit themselves to rigorous questioning, they should alert the public when vote seekers are avoiding it. This pols' ploy is a carefully considered campaign tactic and should be reported as such.

Much of the news reaching voters in a presidential race comes from the national press corps—the television, radio, and news magazine correspondents whose reports reach audiences of tens of millions across the country. This cadre comprises the most experienced political journalists. Their rigorous reporting is born of knowledge and cynicism, presumably in healthy balance. During the course of a long campaign, they usually bring to the surface essential facts about policies and personalities.

Toughness in a reporter is a characteristic politicians may respect, but it's also something they're wary of. The office seeker and the news gatherer are natural adversaries.

Of course, not all reporters are equally skilled or equally aggressive. Candidates and their handlers know this, and are always on the lookout for journalists who might treat them gently. Within the top echelons of the national press corps, those reporters might be scarce, but they're easier to find in the ranks of local news media. So politicians have figured out how to increase their chances of getting soft coverage: they set aside blocks of time for interviews by local journalists, sometimes in person, sometimes via satellite.

For example, during the 1992 Republican National Convention, George Bush scheduled several hours for a series of five-minute interviews by local journalists from around the country who were in Houston covering the convention. This was ideal for Republican campaign planners in several respects: in such a brief format, Bush could filibuster about anything he wanted; the reporter would probably be awed by the prospect of interviewing the president of the United States and so would ask "golly, gee whiz" questions; and local stations would be certain to give prominent play to their "exclusive" with the president, maybe repeating it several times. Some—by no means all—reporters and stations slipped into this trap.

Free, favorable exposure. A campaign manager's dream.

The ethical burden rests with the local news organizations. They must make certain they won't be taken advantage of by the politicians. There's no reason a local journalist can't ask questions just as tough as (and perhaps less cynical than) those coming from a national correspondent.

All news organizations, local or national, must retain control of their own pages or airwaves, even if that means occasionally declining to use some material.

For instance, if during the 1992 campaign, a local TV station was offered a live two-minute interview with Democratic vice presidential nominee Al Gore during the evening newscast, a case could be made for refusing. Two minutes is too short for any substantive give-and-take between interviewer and candidate, and because the interview would be live, the station would give up editorial control. Gore could ignore whatever question was asked, expound on whatever he wanted for the two minutes, then say good-bye. That's closer to free advertising than to a news interview.

Also, local news organizations that decide to cover national stories, such as a presidential campaign, have the obligation to assign reporters possessing the skills discussed earlier in this chapter. Having encyclopedic knowledge about goings-on at the local city hall is fine, but that talent doesn't necessarily mean the reporter can adequately inform local news consumers about national issues or, more significantly, about the local impact of national candidates' proposed policies. If you play the game, you have to play it correctly.

Some journalists' political expertise is a product of their own work in politics. The relatively few reporters who entered the news business after serving as candidates' managers or handlers bring a valuable perspective to their work. But they quickly land in ethical quicksand if they aren't certain where their loyalties lie. As journalists, their allegiance must be to the public, not to their political buddies.

For those who change professions once and stick with their new calling, conflicting interests can be straightened out fairly easily. But those who go back and forth between journalism and politics or government may have severe credibility problems.

These are the "revolving door journalists." They may alternate professions numerous times. If they're doing this as part of a long-term career plan, their loyalties might not be clear even to themselves.

Examining this issue, *Washington Post* reporter Haynes Johnson wrote:

None of this is to suggest that the journalists who enter government are somehow venal. . . . But it does indicate a departure from the generally rigid lines that had existed between press and government, and to some degree an inevitable erosion of the journalist's traditional adversary role when dealing with public officials.[8]

Maintaining that adversarial relationship is important. It shouldn't be sacrificed in the name of enhanced expertise.

NEWS VERSUS TRUTH

A journalist's job is to report the news. Or is it to report the truth? This is more than a semantic quandary. The news and the truth aren't always identical.

The distinction was drawn by Walter Lippmann in his 1922 book, *Public Opinion*.

The hypothesis, which seems to me the most fertile, is that news and truth are not the same thing, and must be clearly distinguished. The function of news is to signalize an event, the function of truth is to bring to light the hidden facts, to set them into relation with each other, and make a picture of reality on which men can act. Only at those points, where social conditions take recognizable and measurable shape, do the body of truth and the body of news coincide. That is a comparatively small part of the whole field of human interest.[9]

Lippmann illustrates his point with an example that, although now dated, underscores a journalistic failing that is by no means obsolete.

There is no defense, no extenuation, no excuse whatever, for stating six times that Lenin is dead, when the only information the paper possesses is a report that he is dead from a source repeatedly shown to be unreliable. The news, in that instance, is not "Lenin Dead" but "Helsingfors Says Lenin is Dead."[10]

In this example the *news* is the report from Helsingfors (the unreliable source) that Lenin is dead. But the *truth* isn't known, because the source is unreliable; maybe Lenin isn't dead. Should the newspaper report the *news*, or wait until it can, with certainty, report the *truth*?

Realities of the news business make compromise essential about this. Sometimes, the truth cannot be absolutely ascertained, but the news is still important enough to be conveyed to the public.

In a major, continuing story, such as the unraveling of the Watergate scandal in the early 1970s, journalists have to decide how much to trust their sources and how much corroboration is necessary. Finally, they must calculate the probability of their story being true and, if they're reasonably certain it is, deliver it to the public.

Waiting to uncover "absolute truth"—whatever that is—means you'll end up publishing monthly, if at all. Ben Bradlee, who was executive editor of the *Washington Post* during the Watergate years, suggested a rigorous but realistic standard: the *best obtainable version* of the truth.

In the Watergate story, this meant not waiting for the improbable event of Richard Nixon admitting he was a crook. Rather, *Post* reporters were to investigate, interview sources, corroborate the sources' information, and present the resulting product to the newspaper's readers. The readers then could decide for themselves if the information was true.

This incremental process of gathering and reporting news should, in most cases, produce a reasonable approximation of truth. But in some instances, what is presented to journalists as news is obviously (or perhaps just apparently) not true. What then?

Consider this hypothetical case. You're a network television correspondent assigned to a presidential campaign. Late one day, Candidate X, whom you're covering, makes a speech, which is the biggest event on that day's schedule and must be the basis for your story for that evening's newscast. The cornerstone of the speech is this attack on X's opponent, Y: "When Candidate Y was governor, he claimed credit for reviving his state's economy, but actually he presided over a net loss of 10,000 jobs in his state."

You have done extensive research about both candidates' records and you know that this charge is absolutely wrong. During Candidate Y's tenure, his state actually saw a net *gain* of 5,000 jobs. Official, undisputed records document this. Moreover, you suspect that Candidate X—or at least his speechwriters—know the truth and have purposely misrepresented Y's record.

How should you report the speech? Should you air a sound bite of X making the charge? Assume it is too late in the day to get a rebuttal from Candidate Y. Should you interject your own research findings, challenging X's job figures? If you do that, have you become Candidate Y's surrogate? Candidate X's supporters certainly will think so.

And even if you could get a comment from Y, and he presents the correct statistics, how is the public supposed to know whom to believe? Should you say in your story, "X is wrong, Y is right?" Once again, X's supporters will accuse you of bias.

In this case, the speech is *news*, but it isn't the *truth*. You can report the news and wash your hands of the whole affair, letting the candidates squabble and the voters fend for themselves. But if your higher obligation is to truth, rather than to mere news, you can report about the speech *and* provide the accurate job statistics.

The issue of allegiance to news or truth is complicated by the question of the propriety of a journalist's explaining the truth, rather than letting news consumers deal with that on their own. If a reporter is supposed to be just a conveyor belt, delivering the daily load of campaign rhetoric and media events, then interpreting the goings-on is inappropriate. But if part of the journalist's job is to make sense out of the often overwhelming amount of information a campaign generates, then some intervention is necessary.

Sometimes a compromise resolution of the problem is possible. A straight news story can be accompanied by a sidebar labeled "analysis" or "commentary" that presents truth as supplement to news. That way, news consumers can decide if they want to rely on part or all of the material provided. But often, campaign schedules and news formats make this difficult to do.

Most journalists don't take lightly any decision to interpret news in a way that might be seen as editorializing, and as a result it doesn't happen often. One notable case arose in 1972, when NBC correspondent Catherine Mackin did a story analyzing some of President Richard Nixon's campaign speeches that attacked Democratic nominee George McGovern. After noting that Nixon's criticisms of McGovern lacked specificity, she went on to say: "On welfare, the President accuses McGovern of wanting to give those on welfare more than those who work, which is not true. On tax reform, the President says McGovern is calling for 'confiscation of wealth,' which is not true."[11]

The White House protested, and NBC executives made Mackin spend a day compiling information to substantiate her report (which she was able to do). But, writes campaign press chronicler Tim Crouse: "The extraordinary thing about her piece was that it was virtually unique. Nobody else who reported on the [Nixon] trip said in simple declarative sentences that Nixon had made demonstrably false accusations about . . . McGovern's programs."[12]

Mackin was perceived by some as a McGovern partisan rather than a disinterested observer, but her decision was simply that the public deserved the truth and would accept her as an honest and intelligent purveyor of that truth.

Of course, in many cases the public doesn't need to be told when a politician strays from the truth. In 1991, for example, when President Bush said race was not a factor in his appointing Clarence Thomas to the Supreme Court, reporters didn't have to tell their audiences that this was untrue. The absurdity of the statement spoke for itself.

PROVIDING ESSENTIAL INFORMATION

Discriminating between news and truth is a complex aspect of the more mundane task of judging what is newsworthy and what is mere froth.

With their insatiable thirst for free exposure, politicians constantly flood journalists with everything from faxed news releases to grandly staged stunts. The more desperate they are for coverage, the more creative—or absurd—they become. For instance, in one Texas judicial race, the would-be judge drove around town on a fire engine, hoping that photographers would find this sight irresistible. He never bothered to explain what driving a fire truck has to do with being a judge. Most news organizations had sense enough to ignore this foolishness. In this instance the candidate lost, but there is no shortage of similarly silly antics.

The ethical issue here is the responsibility of journalists to distinguish between reporting and merely serving as a pass-through mechanism for politician-supplied information. Covering a candidate and promoting a candidacy are two very different businesses.

Coverage decisions should be guided by a determination to provide voters whatever they need to know to cast an informed ballot. Among these basic elements are the following:

— What the job entails. Sometimes voters show up at the polls without knowing what the responsibilities of a particular office are. In Texas, for example, one of the most coveted elected offices is a seat on the state Railroad Commission. The job may sound like a quaintly obsolete sinecure, responsible for counting ca-booses. Actually, it is an extremely powerful post that today has very little to do with railroads but involves supervising the oil and gas industry, regulating trucking, and other crucial responsibilities. In theory, Texans learned about this in high school civics class, but that theory doesn't hold up well. Voters need reminders.

— The voting record or other professional history of the candidates. Incumbents' voting records, campaign finance reports, attendance records, and other relevant documentation should be put in a form that's easy for voters to scrutinize. For instance, without having to decipher the code that some legislative bodies use to record their members' votes, the news consumer should be able to find out whether his or her representative has been showing up for work. Also, even most first-time office seekers have some background germane to the post they want. It may be service on community boards or a record of business accomplishments or failures. Whenever possible—which is most of the time—voters should be spared the pain of postelection revelations (such as the self-proclaimed "success-ful businessman" candidate who turns out to have been jailed for fraud six times).

— Responses to questions about issues. Many news organizations submit issues questionnaires to candidates. This is a useful device; it allows side-by-side comparisons of the office seekers and compels candidates to state positions (or lets voters see that they have offered "No response").

This combination of researching background and eliciting candidates' views can produce a lot of information—more than many voters will wish to ingest. But journalists should provide it and then let news consumers do with it what they will. The journalist's responsibility is not infinite. At some point, it's up to the voters to take advantage of information they've been given.

COVERING THE HOMETOWN CANDIDATE

Special responsibilities arise when local news organizations cover as a candidate someone whom they've covered in other contexts.

A good example of this can be seen in the challenge Dallas news organizations faced when Ross Perot sought the presidency in 1992. Long a public figure, but never before a political candidate, Perot lacked an extensive governmental record such as those of Bill Clinton and George Bush.

Perot had, however, built his multibillion-dollar business empire in Dallas, and had served in quasi-political roles while chairing a state education reform task force and leading a Texas antidrug crusade. He had made much of his money through contract work for the state and federal governments. He also had from time to time devised his own foreign policy, working on behalf of American prisoners of war in Southeast Asia and liberating some of his company's employees from an Iranian jail.

In Dallas, Perot long had been the stuff of legend and controversy. Much information about him was on the record, much was merely gossip.

He was masterful at defining his own image. As a private citizen, Perot could exercise considerable control over journalistic renderings of his persona. For instance, *On Wings of Eagles*, the book (and later television movie) about the Iran jailbreak, was produced with Perot's veto power over the book's author and the movie's cast. (To play Perot, actor Richard Crenna—taller and with smaller ears—was approved.)

In 1992, the task for journalists was to distinguish between Perot's sometimes fanciful self-portrayal and reality. Dallas journalists—especially business writers—presumably had enough background knowledge and sources to tell Perot's story accurately and in detail. Not only would they provide information to their own audiences, but they'd also be relied upon by political reporters who were scrambling to make sense of this out-of-nowhere candidacy.

Not all the tales about Perot were flattering. As he built his computer services company and his personal fortune, his energy and perseverance were inspiring, but he had been accused of employing unethical tactics, particularly when competing for contracts.

On the other hand, Dallas news organizations mirrored civic pride in having a hometown star in the presidential race. Perot and his family were well known for their many local business and charitable interests. He had given millions to civic enterprises, such as the public arboretum and the new downtown concert hall.

A natural temptation—which in this case most Dallas journalists resisted—was to be more booster than reporter, to allow Perot to wear a protective cloak of friendly news coverage, much in the way the Dallas Cowboys enjoyed news media cheerleading as they made their way toward the 1993 Super Bowl.

Such pseudo journalism might make lots of people in Dallas (especially Perot) feel good, but it's intrinsically dishonest. Politicians won't complain on the rare occasions that press bias works in their favor, but politicians aren't the news media's true constituency. The public is, and the public deserves the whole story—the bad as well as the good—about Ross Perot or any other candidate.

As with many other ethical issues, journalists will be on shaky ground if they allow extraneous factors—such as a shared hometown—to influence tone or content of coverage. In major news markets such as Dallas, solid journalism will usually prevail, but this kind of case arises on state and local levels frequently. Whether a big-city TV station or a small-town newspaper, the news organization should maintain its allegiance to its viewers or readers, not to the politicians.

Journalists must stay alert. Bias, incomplete research, cheerleading . . . each can wreck a story if a reporter, editor, or producer is careless. The result: an inferior news product, weakened public trust, and substantial damage to the profession's ethical foundation.

Chapter Three

The Character Issue

Issues. They're the intellectual heart of politics. They're what the voters need to know about. They're what journalists are supposed to explain.

"We'll focus on the issues" is the vow in virtually every newsroom in virtually every campaign. Ideally, it means producing comprehensive, thoughtful analyses of candidates' positions on economic growth, health care, education, defense, the environment, and so on.

Flood the public with substance. They'll dutifully absorb it, make wise voting decisions based on it, and be forever grateful to journalists for providing it.

Hah!

It doesn't work that way. First, issues stories require lots of work—researching in libraries, interviewing experts, assembling data. That's no fun. It's not the run-and-gun reporting that makes politics such an appealing beat.

Also, the public that is being so assiduously served tends to greet such efforts with sustained yawns. Too much emphasis on issues is boring; *people* are more interesting than issues.

Particularly in presidential elections, many Americans cast their votes based on their evaluation of the person rather than because of loyalty to a particular party or issues position. In part, this is a product of voter reliance on television, which brings the candidates into our living rooms, where we can give them the once-over as they amiably try to convince us that they're fine folk.

Survey research from the 1984 presidential campaign found that solid majorities of voters agreed with Walter Mondale rather than Ronald Reagan about issues such as deficit reduction and aid to the Nicaraguan Contras. But when asked whom they wanted to be president, the response was overwhelmingly "Reagan." While not particularly caring for some of his issues positions, they liked *him*.

Similarly, when George Bush realized in 1992 that he would lose if election results were determined by the dominant issue—the state of the economy—he urged voters to support the candidate they thought was the most trustworthy, the best person. The Bush campaign increasingly focused on Bush's virtues and Bill Clinton's alleged lack of such. Instead of addressing the needs of 11 million unemployed Americans, Republicans emphasized Clinton's avoiding the military draft more than two decades earlier.

The determinative issue, according to Bush's handlers, should be "character"—moral fitness to be president of the United States.

In her valuable 1988 book, *Character*, Gail Sheehy acknowledged the potency of this voting issue and profiled that year's presidential candidates (plus incumbent Ronald Reagan), examining the backgrounds that shaped their public lives. Character, she wrote, "is a perceived combination of those traits—together with the values he or she represents—that set a person apart, and motivate his or her behavior."[1]

Sheehy interviewed friends, relatives, teachers—as many as fifty people who had known the candidate at various stages of his life. Then she talked to the candidate himself. The process, she said, "is like working on a psychological thriller."

No set formula exists to guide journalists in defining "character." Some traditional values—such as truthfulness and marital fidelity—are much in vogue, while others—such as churchgoing and successful parenting—are largely ignored (as in the case of Reagan).

Press and politicians engage in a vague dialectic that produces the current standards. Sometimes rumors stimulate press inquiry and a resultant definition of acceptable and unacceptable behavior. This happened after tales of Gary Hart's womanizing had circulated for so long and so widely that journalists felt they had to do something about them.

Also, the candidates themselves can push the press toward a particular measurement of character. In 1992, the Bush campaign's relentless badgering of Bill Clinton about his avoiding Vietnam-era military service was a factor in the news media's giving the topic such prominent play.

Journalists, who are not always paragons of virtue themselves, thus play the odd role of moral arbiter, and do so without firmly rooted or widely accepted principles on which they may rely.

No universally accepted code of journalism ethics exists. Instead of having precise definitions of acceptable and unacceptable ways to gather and report the news, journalists must rely on an array of codes and guidelines, precedent, advice from colleagues, and instinct. That mix does not always produce an enlightened approach to news decisions.

Generally, "character" in a campaign context is linked to fitness to hold office. Will a particular attribute help or hurt performance of public responsibilities? Vague as this criterion may be, it at least serves journalists as justification for their poking, prodding, and pontificating. Of course, one person's scoundrel may be another's saint; whether a candidate is fit or unfit depends on the eye of the beholder.

Beyond problems of vagueness are dangers of being manipulated by pols trying to trash their opponents. Press investigation of a candidate's alleged flaws can screen an opponent who is originating smears. Mere allegations sometimes can do as much damage as solid proof.

For example, in the Democratic primary of the 1990 Texas governor's race, Jim Mattox frequently suggested to reporters that they look into possible cocaine use by Ann Richards. When reporters asked Richards— who has made no secret of being a recovering alcoholic—about it, she refused to answer directly.

Mattox initially didn't want to level the charge himself; he could look relatively pristine if the press did his dirty work. Then, after reporters had opened the door, he could add fuel to the fire by demanding that Richards answer the journalists' queries.

He attacked on two fronts: implying that Richards was a drug abuser, and therefore unfit to lead the state's fight against drugs, and that she was dishonest. Mattox was able to victimize journalists because of their preoc-cupation with "character." They didn't know exactly what they were looking for or what standard they should hold Richards to, but that was fine with Mattox.

No evidence was ever found of Richards having used cocaine or having been treated for any drug problem other than her alcoholism, but the charges clouded the campaign. Reporters covering her seemed to be mem-bers of a snarling wolf pack. Some important state governance issues got short shrift in coverage. Public opinion split: some voters wanted full disclosure from Richards; others resented the intrusion into what they considered to be none of the public's business.

Richards skillfully counterattacked,using television ads to label Mattox a mudslinger. Mattox and much of the press corps looked like villains. Richards went on to win the nomination and the governorship.

This is by no means a unique story. It is part of an established pattern, especially in presidential politics. Long before television brought us "liv-ing-room candidates," the character of the men who would be president was a dominant issue. Impugning an opponent's character has been a much-used tactic throughout the nation's history, and journalistic coverage of this often has left much to be desired.

EVOLUTION OF THE CHARACTER ISSUE

Blame it on Parson Weems. Hagiographer of George Washington, Weems gave us a chopped-down cherry tree and a virtuous young president-to-be whose "I cannot tell a lie" established an early character standard that has haunted other White House aspirants.

Even Washington was not unassailable. The first president was occasionally attacked as being a closet monarchist. Thomas Paine, ancestor of today's partisan columnists, penned a pamphlet labeling Washington "treacherous in private friendship . . . and a hypocrite in public life." Paine continued: "The world will be puzzled to decide whether you are an apostate or an impostor; whether you have abandoned good principles or whether you ever had any."[2]

For Washington, that was unusually rough treatment. But his early successors were regularly pummeled with far greater ferocity. One character test was to measure a politician on a vague scale of ardor for revolutionary principles. Suspected fondness for kings (British or French or, prospectively, American) or other aspects of aristocracy was a fatal flaw in the eyes of some, while other observers dreaded the prospect of "The Marseillaise" becoming America's national anthem. Pamphleteer journalists held John Adams and Thomas Jefferson to whichever of these standards appealed to them.

Purely personal qualities also were the stuff of many character tests. Andrew Jackson married his wife before her divorce was final, so he was loudly proclaimed a bigamist (and, presumably, assailed for his shoddy "family values"). For good measure, his late mother was called a prostitute. His supporters viewed his character in a different light, creating the imagery of "Old Hickory"—common-man farmer (he actually was a slave-holding plantation owner) and heroic soldier.

Neither the positive nor the negative characteristics ascribed to Jackson had much to do with his possible presidency, but campaign strategists—then, as now—understood that voters wanted to know about more than the politics of their politicians. In selecting a president, finding the best man often took precedence over identifying the best policy positions.

Few 19th century politicians were as thoroughly reviled as Abraham Lincoln. According to his opponents, Lincoln was a lying, stupid teller of dirty stories. The invective was directed at his upbringing, his looks, his morals, and his business practices.

Although this vituperation was rooted in opposition to Lincoln's policies—especially those involving slaveholders' rights—many of the accusations made no mention of such matters. They amounted to nothing more than name-calling and addressed only his character.

With the benefit of historical hindsight, we can laugh at such ridiculous attacks on the author of the Gettysburg Address. But at the time, many people listened attentively to the charges and wondered if this Lincoln fellow could be entrusted with the presidency.

If leaders of the stature of Washington and Lincoln had to endure such onslaughts, imagine the assaults on congressional or local candidates.

Savage attacks on character were common elements of political discourse. They were spread, in part, by a press that made up in size and diversity what it lacked in substance and responsibility. Broadsides, pamphlets, and newspapers proliferated.

Their often scurrilous nature was lampooned by Charles Dickens in *Martin Chuzzlewit*, which was published in 1844. As Martin arrived in New York from England, he was greeted by a legion of newsboys touting their papers:

"Here's this morning's New York Sewer!" cried one. "Here's this morning's New York Stabber! Here's the New York Family Spy! Here's the New York Private Listener! Here's the New York Keyhole Reporter! Here's the New York Rowdy Journal! Here's all the New York papers! Here's full particulars of the patriotic loco-foco movement yesterday, in which the whigs was so chawed up; and the last Alabama gouging case; and the interesting Arkansas dooel with Bowie knives; and all the Political, Commercial, and Fashionable News. Here they are! Here they are! Here's the papers, here's the papers!" . . .

"It is in such enlightened means," said a voice almost in Martin's ear, "that the bubbling passions of my country find a vent."[3]

This reasonably depicts the wilder popular press in the mid-19th century. Presumably, editors of the "New York Sewer" would have few qualms about printing the juiciest available items—factual or not—about politicians, raising whatever character issues would sell the most papers.

Damage caused by irresponsibility of this kind was sometimes mitigated by the number and diversity of journalistic outlets. Readers generally knew of publications' political leanings and interpreted their contents accordingly. Residents of large cities or those who got their journalism by mail often could pick and choose to get as narrow or as broad a spectrum of opinion as they desired.

Today, not only irresponsibility but also constructive exuberance are tempered by the notable absence of diverse media voices. In one-newspaper cities—of which there now are many—journalistic passion often yields to the demands of stolid evenhandedness. That may be ethical, but often it's also dull and deadens political debate.

Moving toward and into the twentieth century, the science of mass communications became more refined and the amount of information available to the public steadily grew. But little of substance changed in the way journalists evaluated politicians.

Delving into family matters continued to be standard procedure. In 1912, one of Democratic presidential nominee Woodrow Wilson's daughters said she found "this prying into our lives strange and annoying." Reporters, she said, "did not hesitate to question us about any and every detail of our lives. What were our favorite colors, occupation, sports? Did we like to dance? Were we in love or engaged? Did we intend to marry and, if so, when?"[4]

Pretty tame stuff, but still pointlessly intrusive. Justified as providing insight into Wilson's character, it really was just a way to satisfy perceived public curiosity. It added little to public understanding of Wilson's candidacy.

Personal characteristics can displace issues in forming judgments about politicians. Franklin Roosevelt was always a lightning rod for personal attack. In 1936, *Fortune* magazine took note of this: "For one criticism of New Deal measures you will hear ten criticisms of the presidential voice, the cocksure manner, the gladsome face, the cheerful elusiveness, the happy heart. There is nothing about the man that may not be made the cause of dislike."[5]

Roosevelt also has the distinction of being attacked for being too much of a dog lover. In 1944, he was accused (falsely) of having forgotten his Scottish terrier during a visit to the Aleutian Islands and then sending a Navy destroyer to retrieve the dog. Roosevelt's response was his famous Fala speech:

The Republican leaders have not been content to make personal attack upon me, or my wife, or my sons. They now include my little dog, Fala. Unlike members of my family, Fala resents this. . . . I am accustomed to hearing malicious falsehoods against myself . . . but I think I have a right to object to libelous statements about my dog.

THE ADULTERY QUESTION

Wilson and Roosevelt were among the numerous presidents who were reputed womanizers. This topic has come to epitomize the character issue, and it offers some good examples of how news media standards fluctuate.

Generally kept at the level of a whispering campaign, such rumors traditionally received mainstream press treatment only when the candidate's opponents pushed the matter into the public realm. For example, charges during the 1884 presidential campaign that Grover Cleveland had fathered an illegitimate child received a full airing in the news media. Cleveland, labeled by some editorial writers a "moral leper," admitted to having the affair and to being the father.

Certainly this was a full-fledged scandal—provoking much gleeful disapproval—but voters still thought Cleveland more honest than the Republican nominee, James G. Blaine ("the continental liar from the state of Maine"), and so sent the Democrat to the White House.

More typical was journalists' response to escapades of John Kennedy. Some members of the political press corps (which, until recently, was almost all male) knew about the president's skirt chasing but kept quiet, absent clear evidence of his pleasures interfering with his duties. Presumably, many Americans would have considered Kennedy's behavior evidence of a serious character flaw, but because journalists observed a code of silence, it never became an issue.

After Kennedy's death, his alleged liaison with Judith Campbell Exner came to light. While involved with the president, she also had been a close friend of organized crime boss Sam Giancana. Imagine the political firestorm that would have been ignited had Kennedy lived and had this relationship been revealed during his 1964 reelection campaign.

By adhering to rules (widely observed although unwritten) that excluded from coverage those "character" matters not involving clear-cut corruption or abuse of power, journalists were more White House Praetorian guard than public watchdogs.

That coziness began to dissolve when the adversarial relationship between press and presidents became sharper during the Vietnam War and the Watergate scandal. The press corps grew larger and more aggressive. By the time Richard Nixon resigned in 1974, most of the friendly protectiveness journalists had extended to presidents was gone. New lines had been drawn, new (if still vague) rules established.

How this redefined relationship worked could be seen in the spectacular demise of Gary Hart. After almost knocking off front-runner Walter Mondale in 1984, Hart was the Democrats' most likely 1988 nominee when he announced his candidacy in early 1987.

For years, rumors had floated in political circles that Hart had trouble keeping his pants zipped. The number of reports and the quality of sources gave weight to the tales and precipitated some lengthy newsroom debates about what kind of coverage would be appropriate. The generally accepted "responsible" position: leave the topic alone unless it is relevant as part of a larger analysis of the candidate's fitness for office.

That's nicely ethical, but in the rush of day-to-day journalism what is nicely ethical doesn't always govern what appears in print or on the air. In April, a *Newsweek* profile of Hart stated that he had been "haunted by rumors of womanizing."[6]

If they were merely "rumors," should they have been mentioned? The gossip had fueled many a late-night barroom discussion among political reporters, but no one seemed to have solid proof. When journalists badgered Hart about the topic (devoting considerably more energy to this than to his tax policy), he let his annoyance show and asked if other candidates were leaking the tales to discredit him. News stories then appeared about Hart's response, making him seem guiltily defensive.

At one point, an exasperated Hart told the *New York Times* that reporters could follow him and they'd be bored. They did, and they weren't.

In early May, the *Miami Herald* received anonymous tips from a woman claiming to be the friend of a woman—later identified as Donna Rice—who was having an affair with Hart. After some of the information she supplied was corroborated, *Herald* editors listened carefully when the tipster said that Rice was flying from Miami to Washington to spend the weekend with Hart at his town house.

A *Herald* reporter spotted Rice on the plane and, later, emerging with Hart from the town house. An inexpertly planned stakeout of Hart's house saw Hart and Rice reenter and not come out again until the next day. That, plus a tense confrontation between reporters and Hart, gave the paper ammunition for a story headlined "Miami Woman Is Linked to Hart."

The *Washington Post* then began sifting through its own supply of rumors, including one about a long-lasting relationship between Hart and a woman who was an acquaintance of several *Post* staff members. Allegations about this liaison were accompanied by some circumstantial evidence—photographs from a private detective who had tailed Hart to the woman's home and taken his picture as he left early the next morning.[7] (The detective apparently had been hired by a man who thought Hart was having an affair with the man's wife. But that woman was not the one whom Hart was visiting when the detective snapped the photo.)

While all this was percolating, Hart held a news conference in New Hampshire. The candidate and *Post* reporter Paul Taylor had an exchange that included the following:

Taylor: Do you believe adultery is immoral?

Hart: Yes.

Taylor: Have you ever committed adultery?

Hart: I do not think that's a fair question.[8]

Later that day, *Post* editors received confirmation of the other story from the woman involved. Taylor was assigned to get Hart's reaction. But the candidate was unavailable. The next morning Taylor was told that Hart had gone back to Colorado and was dropping out of the presidential race.[9]

In the wake of Hart's departure from the campaign, debate focused not only on his fidelity and truthfulness but also on the news media's standards.

Robert Caro, biographer of Lyndon Johnson, said, "It's legitimate to know all we can about a candidate. The moral and personal tone a president sets is as vital for the nation as his foreign policy. . . . What's wrong is that we give the sexual revelations such disproportionate weight."[10]

Williams College professor James MacGregor Burns said:

The media aren't able to deal adequately with real and total character; their judgments are based on such old-fashioned, puritanical pieces of evidence. The character question should deal with the totality of a person. How does he treat people? Does he keep his word? Is he wise and fair? How does he handle subordinates? The real humaneness of the man.[11]

And writer John B. Judis offered this commentary:

If the mainstream press is going to report a candidate's philandering or his bedroom behavior, then the press will either have to convince its readers that what it is printing is directly relevant to political life or it will have to suffer the charge of sensationalism and scandal-mongering.[12]

Hart himself warned that the campaign process "reduces the press of this nation to hunters and presidential candidates to being hunted."[13]

These cautionary notes are worth heeding, but aggressiveness should not be replaced by timidity in gathering news. The Hart episode exposed some flaws in journalists' news judgment, but the coverage also exposed significant flaws in this would-be president. His behavior was reckless, and not on just one occasion. This candidate's pattern of irresponsibility—whatever the specifics—may well have foreshadowed problems in his potential presidency. The public had a right and a need to know about that.

Suppose the press had not acted on the rumors about Hart's skirt chasing. Suppose further that he was elected president. Suppose still further that as president he engaged in similarly reckless behavior that embarrassed not only him but the nation. Would journalists then tell the country, "Oh, yeah, we knew that Hart was a flake, but we decided not to report it"?

Few people would be happy about that.

Four years later, another front-running presidential aspirant found that journalists remain very interested in candidates' sex lives.

Arkansas governor Bill Clinton, like Gary Hart, had long been the subject of rumors about his avid pursuit of women other than his wife. The stories had cropped up in various forms during his Arkansas campaigns. They appeared to have had little impact on his home state voters, who regularly returned him to the governor's mansion by comfortable margins.

With a clear lead in fund-raising and organization, Clinton early on was anointed the front-runner in the 1992 Democratic presidential race. And with most party heavyweights scared off by George Bush's Gulf War-based popularity, Clinton cruised easily through the early stages of his candidacy.

Then the vague rumors became a very specific story. In January, as the caucus and primary season was beginning, an Arkansas state employee and singer named Gennifer Flowers told the weekly tabloid *The Star* that she had had a long-term romantic relationship with Clinton. Flowers had previously denied similar stories and had once threatened to sue a radio station that named her as a Clinton girlfriend. Now she released recordings that purportedly implicated Clinton ("the secret love tapes that prove it!" according to *The Star*) but were ambiguous at best. To complicate matters further, Flowers reportedly had been paid at least $40,000 for her story.

With the headline "My 12-Year Affair with Bill Clinton" greeting shoppers in supermarket checkout lines around the country, mainstream media faced a difficult choice: absent proof that they could obtain themselves, ignore the story; or rely on *The Star*'s version and report Flowers's allegation.

Most followed the latter course, and some for good measure tossed in other Clinton womanizing rumors that had even less backing than the Flowers charges. Some, such as *Newsweek*, listed the many inaccuracies in Flowers's story. But the reader skimming this and other news accounts would see big pictures of Bill and Gennifer—and perhaps the wronged wife, Hillary, as well—and assume that with all this smoke, there must be a fire.

This mess was epitomized by a special edition of "60 Minutes," the nation's most-watched news program, that followed the Super Bowl (estimated audience: 100 million, more than the number of voters in the 1988 presidential election). CBS, once the setter of high standards for broadcast journalism, basically had no story of its own but, relying on *The Star*'s report, had its correspondent Steve Kroft grill Bill and Hillary Clinton.

The Clintons tiptoed through the sleaze as best they could, and Kroft looked suitably embarrassed by his mission, but there they all were, talking not about the future of the country—which is everyone's business—but instead about the dynamics of a marriage—which is the business of just two people.

Something is awfully wrong here. News coverage of the Flowers allegations far exceeded the attention reporters had paid to candidates' public records and issues positions. Despite journalists' protests that they found all this distasteful, they seemed in no hurry to climb out of the mud. A sampling of their stories' headlines illustrates their quandary: "Substance Versus Sex" (*Newsweek*); "Moment of Truth" (*Time*); and, perhaps most appropriate, "Media Lemmings Run Amok!" (*Washington Journalism Review*).

Some of the mud sloshed over onto George Bush. As with Clinton, rumors had long circulated about Bush having affairs. A few weeks before the 1988 election, the stock market dropped forty points in an hour because of rumors that the *Washington Post* was about to come out with a story about Bush's alleged adultery.[14] (No such *Post* story appeared.) Some alternative newspapers even published the name of a woman reported to have had a long-standing romantic relationship with Bush.

Not much about this reached voters in 1988, but in 1992 the same rumors surfaced. When asked about them at a news conference, Bush exploded, refusing to discuss what he called "sleaze." The press retreated. Pursuing the story was difficult because, in contrast to Gennifer Flowers, the woman in the Bush case wasn't talking. Also, journalists sensed that the public wasn't in the mood for more of this kind of coverage.

(A last-minute attempt by Republicans to revive the Clinton womanizing story is discussed in Chapter 4.)

BEYOND ADULTERY

Unlike Gary Hart, Bill Clinton survived. Although his campaign approached the edge of collapse, he remained steadfast in his denials of

Flowers's charges and—perhaps more important—never seemed to panic. His campaign treasury and organization were strong enough to see him through the wave of negative publicity.

Most helpful to Clinton was the public's apparent willingness to relegate the candidate's personal life to a spot on the agenda well below the truly dominant issue—the nation's sick economy. If you're out of work, you want a president who will help you get a job. The state of his marriage is far less important to you than the welfare of your own family.

The news media are sometimes slow to appreciate this. Many reporters would rather cover a brawl than a serious issues debate. That was obvious throughout the 1992 campaign. Clinton and the Democrats wisely tried to keep the economy as the paramount issue. A sign posted in Clinton's Little Rock headquarters said, "The economy, stupid," to remind campaigners not to get sidetracked. This issue, not some transient distraction, would determine the election's outcome.

This reminder was needed, because the Bush-Quayle campaign—eager to avoid discussing the economy—did its best to make Clinton's character the dominant issue. The Republicans' logic was simple. They needed an issue on which the voters judged Bush to be stronger than Clinton. GOP polling found two: foreign policy, which few voters cared about, and "trust"—that is, presidential character.

Bush partisans kept up a barrage of charges, some explicit, some implied: that Clinton had profited from unscrupulous real estate dealings in Arkansas; that he had used improper means to avoid the military draft during the Vietnam War and then lied about it; that he "loathed" the military; that he had led antiwar demonstrations in England while a Rhodes scholar at Oxford; and, most outrageously, that on a trip to Moscow during his Oxford days, he had somehow become involved with the KGB, the Soviet intelligence agency.

Clinton was tough and adroit enough to deflect these charges with minimal damage to his election prospects. More harmful, however, than the charges being made was the way they came to dominate the nation's political discourse. This was largely a function of the news media. Journalists battered Clinton day after day with questions about the draft, ignoring other, more newsworthy topics.

For example, one day in California, Clinton held a news conference to announce his endorsement by an impressive array of Silicon Valley computer industry executives. This was worthy of coverage: corporate leaders, many of whom had been Bush supporters, in the nation's most politically potent state were saying that they had given up on Bush's economic efforts and had decided that Clinton offered the best hope for the future of their industry. Much of the day's coverage, however, made passing mention of the endorsement or the economic matters underlying it. Instead, the focus was on Clinton fending off still more questions about the draft.

At issue here is fundamental news judgment. Particularly for television reports, with their rigid time limitations, usually only the single aspect of the press conference that is deemed most newsworthy will reach the public. Certainly, the news audience has a *right* to know about Clinton's alleged draft problems, but the "revelations" that day were mostly a rehash of old news. On the other hand, that audience might believe it has a *need* to know about a significant campaign event concerning the economy.

Those who orchestrate a news organization's coverage must decide which potential stories merit reporting and which can be ignored. At all times, priority should be given to providing information that news consumers need in making informed voting decisions.

The KGB allegations raise different questions. The principal Republican spokesman on the matter, California congressman Robert Dornan, admitted he didn't know if the charge was true. President Bush, when attacking Clinton about this on a nationally televised talk show, admitted "I don't have the facts," but nevertheless implied that Clinton had been a traitor. Clinton denied that he had done anything damaging to his country, and labeled the attacks "sad" tactics of a desperate campaign.

How should the press handle all this? The charges initially came from Dornan during a late night speech in the House chamber. With the election only a few weeks away, simply ignoring even unsubstantiated charges is difficult, so the story was reported but generally given little airtime and few column inches. An argument can be made that even that was too much; that unless Dornan could provide some proof of a KGB connection, the story should not be reported. The danger is this: A lie repeated often enough begins to acquire the color of truth.

When Bush himself became involved, this became a major story. Normally, Bush would rely on campaign surrogates to make such a hardfisted personal attack on Clinton, but in this case he did it himself. That's newsworthy.

But should news reports point out that Bush offered no evidence, or would that be assuming the role of Clinton defender? Journalists want to avoid being labeled as campaign partisans, but they also must be wary about putting the imprimatur of "news" on apparent falsehoods, which may give them the appearance of truth.

Presumably, the president, Dornan, and others involved in this episode knew that reporters captivated by the character issue would readily amplify whatever charges were made, and would be so intent on not appearing biased that they wouldn't criticize the flimsiness of the Republican message.

That's pretty much what happened. Although Clinton defended himself adequately and Bush probably suffered some damage from backlash, the story did dominate news coverage for several days. That meant several days when the economy was not the controlling issue. Any such diversion worked to Bush's advantage.

This underscores the need for news organizations to reconcile their desire to report exhaustively with their obligation to be selective about the attention given to various stories. Being turned aside from substance by politicians' ploys is an ever-present danger.

One way to juggle duties is to be particularly careful about story placement. Put the most important—not the most sensational—stories on page 1 or at the top of the newscast. Stick the less substantial—even if more titillating—material elsewhere. The audience picks up such signals about news items' relative significance.

This requires self-discipline; the temptation is to grab your audience by displaying the flashiest material most prominently. It's tempting, but it's not the right thing to do.

MYSTERY CANDIDATES

The 1992 campaign posed another "character issue" challenge to journalists: How do you cover a suddenly appearing major candidate who has virtually no political or governmental record? Ross Perot's emergence and his rapid ascent in opinion polls made the press devise ways to cover him that would be fair in comparison with coverage of Bush and Clinton. He couldn't be treated as merely a novelty—voter response showed he was much more than that—and he didn't deserve to be roughed up simply because he wasn't a member of the traditional politicians' club.

Decisions about Perot coverage were made more challenging by his immense personal resources, which allowed him to package himself artfully (while claiming to detest such packaging), and his penchant for relying on "new news" talk shows rather than the traditional give-and-take with the political press corps. Further, Perot was never shy about displaying his scorn for journalists and refusing to answer questions he didn't like. He was used to being in charge.

Perot's policy positions, mostly on economic issues, received heavy coverage, and so did his personal history. As a self-made billionaire with a penchant for dramatic patriotic gestures, Perot was an almost mythic figure even before venturing into presidential politics.

To his dismay and disgust, however, Perot found that most journalists are not properly worshipful of rich businessmen. His business practices were scrutinized, revealing his penchant for investigating competitors and personal enemies. His corporation, Perot Systems, reportedly fired and canceled medical benefits of an employee with AIDS. To improve yacht access to his vacation home in Bermuda, he had a fragile coral reef dynamited.

Such revelations so angered Perot that they were probably a major factor in his withdrawal from the race in July. When he relaunched his candidacy in October, he said, "I will not spend one minute answering questions that are not directly relevant to the issues that concern the people." He would decide which issues those were.

Despite his protest, character was a particularly important topic in reporting about the Perot phenomenon. He had never held office, so he had no legislative or executive record. He had led antidrug and education reform efforts in Texas, but these provided scanty background about someone who wanted to be president of the United States. Since no Perot the senator or Perot the governor existed, Perot the person would have to suffice.

As the Perot case illustrates, journalists might have to use a sliding scale in deciding how much weight to give personal character: the less extensive the public record, the greater the need for examination of personal life, and vice versa. Of course the "vice versa" is often ignored; even candidates with substantial public histories find their character becoming the preeminent issue.

SETTING STANDARDS

Given the prevalence of character reporting in political journalism, some questions should be asked before deciding how far to intrude into candidates' lives.

FIRST, is the character-related matter germane; might it affect the politician's ability to perform the duties of office? It can be argued, for example, that Gary Hart's dalliance with Donna Rice met this test because his actions were so reckless that they said something about his judgment and stability. On the other hand, a brief affair that took place in 1970 probably wouldn't have much to do with professional competence in the 1990s. Bill Clinton's behavior while in college probably falls outside the boundaries this test establishes (unless he recently misrepresented his actions).

If, however, other issues are involved—such as conflict of interest (perhaps having an affair with someone seeking government contracts)—then even old incidents might deserve scrutiny now.

SECOND, is the politician's conduct hypocritical? If someone is running as "the defender of the American family" while ignoring responsibilities to his or her own family, then reporting the matter is probably justified. Some politicians notably fail to practice what they preach. That gets press attention. For instance, because Pat Robertson ran for president in 1988 as a champion of rigid moral standards, the fact that his first child had been born ten weeks after his marriage deserved mention.

Hypocritical conduct particularly should be reported if it is persistent, establishing a clear pattern of behavior. Also, if the politician lies about an incident, the public should be told that he or she is a liar. On the other hand, if the issue is addressed obliquely but honestly, reportorial prying should be limited. For instance, Bill and Hillary Clinton admitted that their marriage had had problems, that they had dealt with those problems, and that it was a private matter. No need exists to dig up all the details and pursue this indefinitely as a news story.

THIRD, who is the source of the information? Extraordinary care should be used if any personal attack is made anonymously or by someone refusing to go on the record. Granting confidentiality to a politician intent on smearing a rival is a bad idea. In fact, such an attack may be news in itself. The public should be told who is slinging mud.

Employing these tests—or variations of them—might help journalists avoid the aimless, print-anything approach that turns campaign reportage into a feeding frenzy. These measures won't diminish the flow of information; they'll simply help make coverage more thoughtful, honorable, and useful to news consumers.

Beyond the salacious and scandalous, the character of politicians—including influences dating back long before their public careers—may shed light on their performance in office. Some examples from the 1992 presidential campaign:

— The father of candidate Tom Harkin was a coal miner, which helped shape the senator's sensitivity to labor issues.

— Bob Kerrey's Vietnam experiences (losing a leg and winning the Congressional Medal of Honor) would presumably affect his presidential decisions about sending American forces into combat.

— Paul Tsongas's struggle with cancer changed his opinions about government support of medical research and his outlook on life in general.

These are personal matters, but the public needs—and has a right—to know about their potential impact on a presidency. In all these cases, the candidates were more or less willing to reveal their stories, but reporters should press ahead to make certain that they get as much information as the public needs to have.

For example, Tsongas did not reveal a reoccurrence of his cancer, initially claiming that he had been cancer-free since a 1986 bone marrow transplant, but later admitted that more lymphoma had been found in 1987.

Private though illness may seem, this information was not outside the bounds of press inquiry; it related directly to his ability to perform presidential duties. Also, and less speculatively, its timely disclosure might well have affected the race for the Democratic nomination. If the true state of Tsongas's health had been known before the New Hampshire primary (which he won), other candidates might have fared better and been in a stronger position to challenge Clinton.[15]

All these personal background matters should be explored by the press. Doing so doesn't require amateur psychoanalysis, just some thoughtful examination of the past and how it might affect the present and the future.

A related issue is the extent to which candidates' spouses should be the subject of press scrutiny. Traditionally, they have received relatively soft coverage. An exception was John Zaccaro, husband of 1984 Democratic vice presidential nominee Geraldine Ferraro. His business dealings became a major campaign issue and a problem Ferraro had to spend much time addressing. Sexism can reasonably be suspected as a factor in that sudden surge of interest in a candidate's spouse, but regardless of the gender of the candidate, this aspect of campaign coverage merits careful planning.

Standards are changing. In 1992, Hillary Clinton and, to a lesser extent, Barbara Bush attracted significant coverage. Clinton clearly was not planning to be the traditional "political wife." Her reputation as an attorney and her outspoken positions on public issues made it seem—correctly, as it turned out—that she would play a major role in a Bill Clinton administration. So her law review articles and public utterances were examined by reporters. Some of this was done thoughtfully, while some stories clearly reflected reporters' puzzlement about how to treat a strong, independent female professional who was playing such a prominent part in a presidential race.

On the other hand, Barbara Bush may have been undercovered. Her standings in opinion polls remained far above those of her husband, and she was used as a major strategic force in the Republican campaign. She, however, was still generally perceived as a traditional First Lady, and so didn't receive the rigorous scrutiny Hillary Clinton got.

Journalists are looking for a nonsexist standard to use in the future. If the spouses play a major independent campaign role, and if their own issues positions become subjects of campaign debate, then they're likely to get more careful, substantive coverage than they have in the past.

Other family members may also merit coverage. Common sense should lead reporters away from bothering young children, such as Chelsea Clinton in 1992. But if the relatives are adults active in public matters, then they are fair game. For instance, George Bush's son Neil had been involved with a shady S&L. Since S&L corruption and bailouts were major issues affecting his father's administration, the public had a right to know about this. In the 1970s, when Jimmy Carter's brother Billy was just a joke-spouting, beer-drinking good ol' boy, he didn't deserve much hard news coverage. When, however, he registered as an agent for the Libyan government, things changed.

But even when Neil Bush or Billy Carter ought to be covered, journalists should not go overboard. In 1980, the *Washington Post* published more than 100 stories about the Carter case,[16] which eventually proved to deserve much less attention.

One question that might be asked is, Does the relative's activity influence the officeholder's job performance or affect public policy? If not, coverage should not be frenzied. Newsworthiness, as always, should be the standard. Billy Carter did not merit 100 stories.

The character issue will always be with us. Public curiosity and public need to know combine to make stories about character sought-after commodities.

In future campaigns, the character issue should be forthrightly addressed with carefully planned coverage. Background—especially those formative influences that Gail Sheehy examined—should be studied for signals about the aspiring officeholder's likely performance on the job.

Plenty of information is usually available. When people run for office, they implicitly approve the inspection of the nooks and crannies of their lives. Tax returns, campaign finance reports, and other such documents are now either required by law or commonly expected to be furnished by candidates. In light of the Tsongas case, medical records should be added to the list.

In all instances, germaneness should be the guiding standard. Whether sifting through material provided by the campaigner or digging up information independently, reporters should do more than merely swamp the public with everything they acquire.

Also, even a politician is entitled to some privacy; not as much as the average citizen, but some. Respecting privacy is consistently one of the most challenging ethical tests for journalists, whether the story requires interviewing a victim of tragedy or stalking a presidential candidate.

Selectivity is crucial. Well-informed judgments must be made not only about what the public has a *right* to know, but also about what it has a true *need* to know.

That should be the essence of political journalists' approach to the character issue.

Chapter Four

On the Bus

The boys on the bus; more recently, the boys and girls on the bus. This is the press corps that is such a large part of a political campaign's traveling circus.

Today, in presidential races at least, "the boys and girls on the plane" is more apt, as candidates wing from airport news conference to airport news conference. Buses are needed only for those short hauls from airport to city center that are increasingly obsolete. If the TV cameras will come to the airport and relay the candidate's message to the millions watching evening newscasts, then the downtown rallies—even those attended by tens of thousands—become superfluous except as showy displays of public enthusiasm.

The campaign plane or bus (or occasionally train) is a wellspring of camaraderie and competitiveness. The players—politicians and journalists alike—are skilled, ambitious men and women at the tops of their professions. The life-style is a political junkie's dream: every day—and they are long days—is filled with cheering throngs and inside gossip and tidbits of history.

Emerging from these frantic days is a news product, the print and electronic versions of events that fuel the democratic process. The public, however, rarely sees what goes into the making of this product—the constraints of pack journalism and schedules, the relationships between pols and reporters, the judgments about which candidates and events to cover. These behind-the-scenes complexities create a range of ethical issues worth addressing.

PACK JOURNALISM

News coverage of politics has expanded to levels many people consider ridiculous. For instance, the 1992 Democratic National Convention was attended by 4,928 delegates and alternates. Press credentials were issued to approximately 15,000 persons. With even the smallest television stations now having relatively inexpensive access to satellite technology, that latter number probably will continue to grow.

And on any given day after the conventions, the press corps following George Bush or Bill Clinton was sure to number in the hundreds.

The line between comprehensive news gathering and wastefulness is often hard to perceive. News organizations' financial managers search diligently for it. Although economic concerns about pack journalism are important, they shouldn't overshadow ethical issues.

The pack's size itself creates difficulties. Sometimes, many reporters can't get close enough to the candidate to see or hear what is going on. On important occasions, a small pool of journalists is given access and is responsible for telling colleagues what happened. For instance, the pool or the campaign staff will make available audiotapes or verbatim transcripts of the candidate's remarks.

Even when the pool system is working smoothly, many reporters are forced to rely on information gathered by others. This generally doesn't cause problems; competition gives way to "we're all in this together." But before passing on to the public any news that comes secondhand, special care should be taken to corroborate it.

In his landmark book, *The Boys on the Bus*, Tim Crouse described the pack phenomenon this way: "A group of reporters were assigned to follow a single candidate for weeks or months at a time, like a pack of hounds sicked on a fox. Trapped on the same bus or plane, they ate, drank, gambled, and compared notes with the same bunch of colleagues week after week."[1]

This enforced closeness does more than breed irascibility. It fosters consensus journalism. As Crouse describes it: "They all fed off the same pool report, the same daily handout, the same speech by the candidate; the whole pack was isolated in the same mobile village. After a while they began to believe the same rumors, subscribe to the same theories, and write the same stories."[2]

So one reporter's story becomes everybody's story. Conformity is encouraged, while enterprise reporting—breaking out of the pack to get the story no one else has found—is implicitly discouraged.

If the pack is on the right trail, no harm is done. But suppose the collective wisdom of the pack is wrong, and no member of the pack chooses to challenge it. The public gets an inferior news product. An example: In 1984, according to conventional wisdom within the pack covering early stages of the Democratic presidential race, it was a two-man contest. Walter Mondale was presumed the front-runner and John Glenn was seen as the only contender who might have a chance to beat the former vice president. The other half-dozen or so candidates were deemed not worth much bother.

That was how the race was presented to the public. Only Mondale and Glenn received consistent coverage from major news organizations.[3]

But while the pack remained fixated on the campaign as they had defined it, another candidate—Gary Hart—was getting voters' attention. The pack ignored him. Then Hart surprised the press corps by finishing second in the Iowa caucuses, and truly astounded pundits when he walloped Mondale in the New Hampshire primary. Glenn received a total of 13 percent of the vote cast in those two states.[4]

Pack journalism increases the likelihood that reporters will develop tunnel vision. With little incentive to do otherwise, the individual journalist will not look beyond the campaign's boundaries as defined by the pack. In this 1984 example, Glenn's problems weren't invisible; for one thing, his campaign was being badly managed. But as the pack moves through the campaign, it develops an inertia that any individual reporter will have trouble escaping. In fact, an industrious correspondent who proposed a story about Hart as a significant challenger might well have been told by his or her editor, "Nobody else is writing about that," and been sent back to watch Mondale and Glenn.

Eventually, of course, the pack had to dump Glenn and pursue Hart. But the initially narrow focus born of the pack's self-defined conventional wisdom shortchanged the public by not offering an appropriately broad spectrum of reporting. Journalists don't like to take risks and then turn out to have been wrong. And if they are proved wrong, they like to have plenty of company. That's part of why the pack mentality endures. (More about this later in this chapter, in sections about the screening process and expectations.)

So the ethical mandate that emerges from all this is to make sure that uniformity of coverage isn't cheating news consumers. The journalist's responsibility is not to provide *all* available information. Doing so is neither possible nor sensible. But given that selectivity is necessary, reporters should beware of the narrowness of the pack's vision. They should simply keep their eyes open and maintain an appropriately broad view of the campaign, noting all that is going on and making *independent* judgments about what is newsworthy.

TYRANNY OF THE SCHEDULE

When a campaign is in full swing, the candidate tries to cover as much ground and garner as much exposure as possible every day.

Some candidates have the stamina to put in twenty-hour days week in and week out, as was the case with Bill Clinton in 1992 (although his voice periodically vanished). Candidates and their managers set the pace. Journalists have to keep up.

Controlling the schedule often means controlling the news. This happens in many ways:

— When campaign managers have an event or announcement that they particularly want covered, they schedule it early in the day, to make certain reporters have plenty of time to do stories about it. If, on the other hand, something is happening that the managers would prefer to see get scant coverage—for example, an announcements of a staff shake-up—they'll schedule it close to correspondents' deadlines, hoping it will be too late for that day's reports and by the next day will be discarded as "old news." This is sometimes called "the squeeze play."

— Managers try to match what they think will be the most beneficial sound bite of the day with the most appealing visual backdrop of the day. Recognizing television crews' insatiable hunger for "good video," the scheduler can almost guarantee the content of the day's TV reports about the campaign by providing one irresistible media event and having the candidate use it to deliver the message of the day. For instance, national candidates campaigning in Texas are sure to be found making pronouncements about defense policy while standing in front of the Alamo. The symbolism may be cloying, but it usually gets on the air. This scheduling gambit isn't as effective in influencing print reporters, but almost all campaigns are far more concerned about shaping TV coverage.

— Managers may cram the schedule with events to keep reporters from having time to do sidebar analysis or investigative research. A common complaint from members of the traveling press corps is "We don't have time to think." Cover an event, get on the motorcade bus, cover another event, back to the motorcade, onto the plane for a short hop to more events, more motorcades, more flights. . . . This becomes a dizzying carousel ride, whirling so fast that you hold on for dear life rather than try to grab the brass ring. Politicians like this pace in part because they assume a dizzy reporter is a docile reporter. They're probably right, so news organizations should take countermeasures.

For instance, assume candidate George Bush on a given 1992 campaign day has a hectic, crowded schedule. One of his appearances is a speech to a politically powerful African-American organization. The schedule is such that reporters covering Bush must leave the event the instant he has finished speaking if they are to make it to the bus and get to his next stop.

So standard reports about the speech will be basically "Bush said such-and-such and received a whatever response." This probably will suit Bush's managers; they'll hope for minimal coverage of any event at which Bush gets a less than enthusiastic reception.

An editor or producer, however, might decide that the news consumer should learn more about Bush's appeal to a voting bloc that is presumed to be unfriendly to his candidacy but could save him if enough of its members break away from the Democrats. To find out about this, a second reporter should be assigned—someone who need not worry about racing to get on the bus, but instead can stay at the site and talk to audience members about their reactions to Bush. That's the substantive story. Not every news organization has the personnel to double-team events this way, but such measures are necessary to limit the politicians' influence on what is covered and how it's covered.

The principal ethical obligation for journalists in such situations is to resist manipulation, but that has its limits. Campaign managers aren't going to redesign their schedules to help reporters do their jobs better. After all, the pols' definition of good journalism is coverage that makes their candidate look good. Couple this with the sophisticated knowledge most campaigners have about the news business, and a decisive imbalance becomes likely.

The best way to reassert reportorial independence is to plan coverage based not solely on what the campaigners are doing, but also on the journalists' own determination of what the public needs to know.

For instance, during the 1988 presidential campaign, the television networks usually assigned their top political reporters to travel with candidates Bush and Dukakis. On most days that meant coverage content was dictated by the candidate's schedule—making the "event of the day" (as determined by the pols) the dominant imagery of the report that would appear on the nightly newscast.

The candidate could say as much or as little as he chose about the issue of his choice. The correspondents were stuck with that because they had to report about *something*. The Bush campaign was particularly adroit, using flag-wrapped backdrops to cast the candidate as the all-American hero. The high point (or perhaps low point) of such efforts came when Bush toured a flag factory. It was the quintessential photo op—the candidate awash in red, white, and blue.

But, stripped of subtlety, symbolism can become parody. Many reporters had sense enough to point out the brazenness of this attempt to manipulate voters' patriotic emotions.

Sometimes reporters feel trapped by the grotesqueries of media events. Considering the tastelessness of a candidate's—and the press corps's—visit to a neonatal intensive care unit, one reporter wrote in his memoir of the campaign: "We stand there all thinking the same thing: What the hell are we doing here? Why is this necessary? And when will either the press or the candidates develop some sense of shame?"[5]

Television's emphasis on "good video" often conflicts with substantive political discourse. Pictures are more highly valued than what is said. Kiku Adatto's study comparing the presidential campaigns of 1968 and 1988 found the following: during weekday evening network newscasts, "the average 'sound bite' fell from 42.3 seconds in 1968 to 9.8 seconds in 1988. Meanwhile the time the networks devoted to visuals of the candidates, unaccompanied by their words, increased more than 300 percent."[6]

Further, "It was not uncommon in 1968 for candidates to speak uninterrupted for over a minute on the evening news (21 percent of the sound bites); in 1988, it never happened."[7] On the network newscasts, "Bush and

Dukakis got to speak for 30 seconds or more only 15 times during the 1988 general election campaign, compared to 162 times for Nixon and Humphrey in 1968."[8]

Rather than letting viewers hear what the candidates had to say, TV news relied on images carefully designed by the candidates' managers. "So attentive was television news to the way campaigns constructed images for television that political reporters began to sound like theater critics, reporting more on the stagecraft than the substance of politics."[9]

This interjection of journalists' personas sometimes can enhance the analytical nature of their stories, but often it just adds clutter. Giving news consumers significant portions of the candidates' unadulterated stump speeches (as some news organizations do) encourages voters to make up their minds without journalists' help.

The two approaches are not mutually exclusive. But recent coverage trends favor the reporter-dominated story. The spectrum of offerings should be broadened.

Coverage of the candidates' road shows not only lacks substance but also displaces research-based stories about issues. The star reporters' work will be aired, even if they're merely chasing around the country in the candidates' wake. Perhaps their time would be better used—and the voters would be better served—if field producers or junior reporters were assigned to most of the day-to-day travels and the journalistic stars spent their time in pursuit of substance.

For instance, in 1988 Dukakis's record as governor and Bush's performance as vice president were the best indicators of what kind of president each might become. Did Dukakis really work economic miracles in Massachusetts? What was Bush's role in making Reagan administration policy? If reporters had spent more time in Boston and Washington, rather than on the campaign bus, maybe such questions would have been answered more thoroughly.

In postmortems after the 1988 campaign, many journalists acknowledged that they and their coverage had been manipulated. Steve Friedman, executive producer of "NBC Nightly News," said, "We were captives of the bus. We got sucked in. I don't think we examined anything except what the candidates were doing."[10]

During the 1992 race, news organizations worked harder to assert their primacy as agenda shapers and arbiters of truthfulness. Writing a few weeks before Election Day, Alan Otten of the *Wall Street Journal* noted, "The network news programs are conscientiously ignoring most of the photo ops the candidates so carefully stage, and on the rare occasion the networks do carry one, they usually accompany it with balancing or even deflating analysis."[11] And Susan Zirinsky, CBS News political editor, said, "We're not afraid *not* to be on the bus. We've stepped back. We don't do 'the day.' We look at issues."[12]

This self-congratulation makes journalists feel good, and it is not entirely undeserved. But even in 1992, candidates staged some media events that proved irresistible. Most notable were the Clinton-Gore bus tours, especially the first two following the Democrats' convention. Although the candidates and their managers knew they could directly reach far more voters by jetting around the country, they calculated that the real value of these trips would be the indirect voter contact provided by news coverage. They were right; most stories ranged from merely positive to unabashedly adulatory.

Local media were particularly enthusiastic. Some stations went so far as to preempt "Family Feud" and "The Price Is Right" to make room for live coverage as the Democrats' buses rolled through town. For example, in Eau Claire, Wisconsin, the *Leader-Telegram*'s front page headline was "Bus Tour Drawing Accolades. Rural Areas Get Rare View." This was accompanied by color photographs covering much of the page. The next day's headline was "Clinton Says Voters Need 'Courage.' " And the day after that, the same paper included seven articles about the candidates' visit plus a full page of photos.[13]

Even some members of the national press corps were impressed. Joe Klein wrote about "the emotional connection [between candidates and public] that mocked and then demolished the industrial-strength cynicism of the 150 journalists tagging along."[14] And Michael Kelly noted, "Isolated on buses, exposed to mile after mile and hour after hour of cheering Clinton supporters, even the national reporters tend to respond with positive stories."[15]

These results were not accidental. Clinton staff members knew what they were doing. Understanding that the public was favorably disposed to Clinton after the convention, the Democrats' strategists wanted to use news reports to amplify the good feelings. They calculated correctly that national and local press coverage would reflect the Norman Rockwell-like look and mood of small-town America.

The bus tours had some news value, so the press can't be said to have been suckered into covering a worthless media event. Nevertheless, journalists should recognize the attempts at exploitation inherent in any such extravaganza. Being alert will limit the pols' success at manipulating coverage.

While journalists worry abut such matters, technological advances are creating new ethical challenges, particularly for television.

Using satellites and other whiz-bang tools, television networks and—increasingly—local stations can bring live coverage to their viewers. Campaign events can be covered in progress. Candidates can offer their latest comments about the controversy of the moment.

But for news organizations to feature this immediacy requires a trade-off: considerable editorial control may be surrendered. Candidates may

offer unproven claims about their own achievements or level unsubstantiated charges against opponents. If it's live, the TV producers and reporters
have no ability to screen what viewers get—no time to check facts or get
immediate rebuttals. The politician is in command.

As tempting as it may be for journalists to use all the gimmicks at their
disposal, some restraint is called for. As with choosing which events from
the daily campaign circus performance are worth relaying to the public, so
news organizations should carefully select live spots to ensure balanced,
complete reporting.

For instance, if a candidate is to be interviewed live, have the opponent
also on the air. Mini-debates are better than one-sided pronouncements. Or,
if that's not possible, at least have a knowledgeable political reporter on
hand to spot any glaring misstatements by the candidate and point them
out to viewers.

The campaign schedule does affect coverage; that's unavoidable. Nevertheless, journalists have an ethical obligation to prevail over the politicians in the tug-of-war about what gets reported. Failure to do so will
inevitably mean that voters will have to base their balloting decisions more
on froth than on substance.

LAST-MINUTE TRICKERY

As Election Day draws nearer, voters pay more attention to political
coverage. Final decisions about whom to support are fueled by candidates'
frantic flurries of travel and advertising, and by journalists' efforts to make
sense of a year's worth of campaigning.

Give-and-take among candidates eventually stops, but sometimes a
politician's final-hour desperation creates a difficult ethical dilemma for the
press corps.

Consider this case. On November 2, 1992—the day before the election—the following document was faxed to news organizations around
the country. It was a transcript of remarks by Michigan Congressman Guy
Vander Jagt, chairman of the National Republican Campaign Committee:

There have been persistent rumors in Washington that Bill Clinton is currently
having an affair with a member of the traveling press that has been covering him
on this Presidential campaign.

While I have been traveling today, the NRCC, of which I am the chairman,
received a phone call from a member of the Secret Service covering Bill Clinton to
tell us that this is a fact.

I believe—even at this late hour—it is incumbent on the nation's media to find
out if it is true.

If it is not true, it ought to be exposed as the rumor that it is. . . .

If you are an editor or news director, what do you do when you receive this document? If you're editing a daily newspaper, your options are varied:

— You can make a big deal about it, with a headline such as "New Charges About Clinton Infidelity."
— You can make it a major story, but approach it from another angle: "Republicans Try Last-Minute Smear of Clinton."
— You can report the "rumor" and say it appears to be unfounded.
— You can downplay the story, including Vander Jagt's remarks as a minor part of a pre-election wrap-up.
— You can publish nothing about it.

The difficulty in choosing what to do arises partly because of the timing. Your coverage will appear on Election Day. You don't have time to verify it independently. The journalist with whom Clinton supposedly has been having the affair is unnamed. The fax says the Secret Service agent "has requested anonymity." Given the timing, Clinton probably will have no chance to rebut the charge. And even if he does, his rebuttal—no matter how forceful—is likely only to make the story more prominent.

So you have an unsubstantiated attack that is sensational enough to affect the outcome of a presidential election. If your newspaper is widely circulated in a swing state, the story could cost Clinton crucial electoral votes. Or, to raise the stakes, if instead of being a newspaper editor you're the executive producer of a network television newscast, your story could affect millions of votes throughout the nation.

If the story is true—or even might be true—shouldn't voters be told about it before they cast their ballots? If the story is false—or even might be false—shouldn't it be withheld from voters as a matter of fairness?

Vander Jagt's strategy was clear. He presumably was hoping the press would at the very least mention the existence of the "rumor." Doing so might have been enough to influence some undecided voters who had doubts about Clinton's integrity. And if Vander Jagt were later criticized, he could say, "I just suggested that the news media expose this scurrilous untruth."

As it happened, the Vander Jagt ploy was largely ignored by the news media. It was seen by most journalists who learned about it as being an underhanded effort to use the press in a last-ditch attempt to save the Bush campaign.

As this case indicates, sometimes the most ethical thing to do is nothing. News coverage is so influential that its impact must be carefully considered in cases such as this. Merely reporting a rumor gives it the imprimatur of truth. In the Vander Jagt case, many news consumers would assume that if a respected news organization told them about this story, it must have at least some factual basis. That's a reasonable assumption.

Politicians' scruples being what they are, last-minute efforts to shake up the electorate should be expected. As Election Day draws near, journalists should be increasingly on guard against being used.

In another 1992 case, the *Washington Post* was working on a story about accusations that Senator Bob Packwood of Oregon had sexually harassed at least ten women. The accusations were not known to the general public, and the *Post*, which began its investigation in early October, did not publish its report until November 22, almost three weeks after Packwood had been narrowly reelected.

When asked why the *Post* hadn't brought the charges to voters' attention before Election Day, executive editor Leonard Downie, Jr., wrote: "The answer is that on Election Day we still needed to do much more reporting, writing and editing before we had a story sufficiently full, accurate and fair to publish. We wanted to publish as quickly as possible, but not before the story was truly ready." Among the tests the *Post*'s editors felt had to be met, wrote Downie, were these: "Is our reporting complete enough? Is there something important we still don't know? Do we sufficiently understand the pattern and meaning of the facts we have pieced together?"[16]

These are questions worth asking. In the Vander Jagt-Clinton case, as with the Packwood story, they couldn't possibly have been answered overnight. They illustrate an important press responsibility: Don't rush to judgment; get the facts first.

WHERE TO STAND—ON STAGE OR OFF

In their study of presidential campaigns, Nelson Polsby and Aaron Wildavsky concluded:

What we see most often is behavior that is not essentially manipulative or conspiratorial but mutual and interactive. The media and the candidates depend on each other for news to report and for favorable reporting to such a degree that each anticipates the actions and reactions of the other. Observers are correct in noting the extent to which the media are not merely part of the campaign, but centrally important to the campaign.[17]

But as the Vander Jagt case cited above illustrates, pressures exists that might push journalists toward being participants in, rather than merely reporters of, events. Consider the importance of the decision to deliver or withhold news. To decide is to participate. When the attempt is as transparently manipulative as Vander Jagt's was, resistance is easy. But other temptations may be more subtle.

Journalists understand their own power and know that they play an essential role in the electoral process. They can help make or break candidacies by giving or withholding coverage. They tell the public which issues are important and which candidates are worth considering. While doing all this, they become close to those they cover. Ethical danger arises when that closeness breeds a sense of loyalty to the subjects rather than to the recipients of coverage.

Picture this process as taking place within a theater. The politicians are on stage; the voters constitute the audience. Where should the news media be?

The simple answer is, with the public. But influence and closeness may tempt journalists to climb onto the stage and join the players.

Doing this can create numerous ethical problems. At the very least, coverage may become laden with the jargon and allusions of political insiders as journalists forget who their principal audience should be.

Also, closeness may cause reporters, not wanting to upset or damage their pals, to pull their punches. Complex motives come into play. If one of these pals ends up as president, the reporter who has been covering him or her for months might well be assigned to the prestigious White House beat. When a candidate wins, his or her press corps wins, too.

Although news coverage does, unavoidably, influence voting behavior, that influence generally should not be wielded with an eye to a particular electoral outcome. It should happen merely as a matter of course that the public acts on the information with which it is provided.

POLITICIANS AS FRIENDS AND ADVERSARIES

How close should reporters get to the subjects of their coverage? Close enough to acquire good information, while remaining far enough away to ensure independence.

That's a nice answer, but the two parts may be mutually exclusive. If reporters position themselves close enough to their subjects to receive a steady stream of inside information, they're probably so close that their objectivity will be endangered.

For all the talk about the adversarial relationship between press and politicians, cases abound of news professionals who've become so friendly with candidates and officeholders that their work has looked more like public relations than journalism. And in some cases, reporters have suppressed news that might damage their politician friends.

Much of this has involved information about the politicians' personal lives (detailed in Chapter 3). Compared with today's standards, reporters' reticence in some of those cases seems tantamount to cover-up. More charitably viewed, perhaps it merely reflected decisions that even public figures deserve some privacy.

But beyond titillating tales of John Kennedy's alleged bed-hopping are examples of news coverage being shaped by friendship toward one candidate or antipathy toward another. These instances have little to do with personal privacy.

In part these relationships are products of carefully considered strategy decisions by campaign staff. Some pols think it important to cultivate the press; others think they'll be better off treating them as the enemy. The 1960 presidential campaign offered good examples of both approaches.

According to Theodore H. White, John Kennedy

likes newspaper men and likes their company. Kennedy would, even in the course of the campaign, read the press dispatches, and if he particularly liked a passage, would tell the reporter that he had —and then quote from its phrases, in an amazing performance of memory and attention. . . . He would ask advice of newspaper-men—which, though he rarely followed it, flattered them nonetheless.[18]

White also reported that without doubt, "this kindliness, respect and cultivation of the press colored all the reporting that came from the Kennedy campaign." And, writes White, by the end of the campaign, journalists covering Kennedy "had become more than a press corps—they had become his friends and, some of them, his most devoted admirers."[19]

Along similar lines, David Broder—who covered the 1960 campaign for the *Washington Star*—says "Kennedy converted a portion of the press corps covering him into a cheering section." This, says Broder, was the method of seduction:

I was often drawn into conversations in which Kennedy, with extraordinary detach-ment, would dissect the vagaries of his and Nixon's campaign; discuss in bawdy, familiar terms the political and personal strengths and weaknesses of important figures in both parties; and in general, carry on very much as if he were one of us covering the campaign.[20]

On the other hand, in the Republican presidential effort, journalists' "craftsmen's pride in their calling," says White, "was abused by Mr. Nixon and his staff—and not by accident, but by decision. The brotherhood of the press was considered by Mr. Nixon and his press staff, not a brotherhood, but a conspiracy, and a hostile conspiracy at that."[21]

Nixon's press secretary, Herbert G. Klein, later wrote:

The combination of the two things—obvious Nixon enmity toward the press and Kennedy cultivation of the press—had an effect on campaign reporting and on public reaction, and thus it affected the results of a close election. . . . One would have to conclude that Kennedy played the situation well. Neither Nixon nor the press handled the situation as they should have —to understate the case. Nixon must share the blame fully.[22]

The 1960 case is by no means unique. Many candidates, with varied success, long have tried to win the hearts and minds of reporters. Others have felt it beneath them to woo the press corps.

In 1992, Bill Clinton's treatment of the press was similar to John Kennedy's approach. He capitalized on his kinship with reporters. Observing the relationship, Howard Kurtz wrote:

At 45, Clinton was a member of their generation, and he clearly loved the game of politics, just as the reporters did. He spoke their language. He would stroll to the back of the plane and chat about solutions to government problems, joining a debate that neoliberal journalists had been conducting for years.

Kurtz noted that "some journalists grew overly protective of Clinton," but argued that this did not necessarily skew overall coverage.[23] Tough reporting about Gennifer Flowers, the draft, and other matters detrimental to Clinton's candidacy showed that most reporters won't let friendly feelings stand in the way of a good story.

For journalists, the ethical requirement in such instances is one of intellectual discipline: to recognize courtship and not be swayed by it. This doesn't mean, however, imposing an absolute ban on off-the-record contacts with politicians. That might seem ethically pure, but it also may mean missing out on the after-hours gossip and informal bull sessions that contain valuable nuggets of information.

The line between gathering news and being manipulated can become indistinct. Consider this hypothetical: You're the White House correspondent for a major news organization. The president invites you to play tennis with him. Should you do it? Or the president invites you and two or three colleagues to the family quarters of the White House for an after-hours drink. Should you accept? The understanding in both cases is that anything said by the president will be totally off the record.

Motive is important. Few presidents view journalists with anything other than disdain, tempered perhaps by respect for the news media's influence and masked by pseudofriendliness aimed at getting gentler coverage. Their social invitations to journalists are usually part of a strategy to soften up reporters, to make them like the politician enough to put a favorable spin on a story about a presidential speech, or to refrain from taking a critical shot at a presidential program. The thinking is that you might be quick to criticize a politician, but not a tennis partner.

Given that kind of motivation on the part of the president or whoever on his staff recommended this display of bonhomie, your instinct might be graciously to decline the invitation and remove yourself from temptation.

But suppose during the tennis match or the cocktail hour the president says interesting things about Congress, foreign leaders, or other important topics. Even if you couldn't use that material—remember, all this is off the record—you'd be gaining important insight into how he does his job. You would be learning things that neither you nor the public (nor your journalistic competitors) would be likely to glean from the president's public pronouncements. This could be invaluable background for future, on-the-record encounters.

So, even putting aside the alluring glamour of White House socializing, the choice isn't easy. Are you setting yourself up for manipulation, or are you doing your job effectively? If journalists ponder that question carefully, any answer they arrive at probably will be ethically acceptable.

LEAKS AND SOURCES

Information may seem to flow in a steady stream from the news media to the public. But before that happens, journalists must gather the news, sift through it, and then decide what is accurate and important enough to deliver to news consumers. The ways reporters get the pieces of information that become "the news" vary greatly.

Some of it arrives in straightforward fashion. The candidate gives a speech and journalists report what he or she said. But much news travels a more circuitous path. Unlike a speech text or news release, it isn't neatly packaged and presented giftlike to the press corps. Instead, news is often assembled like a jigsaw puzzle, with pieces extracted from nooks and crannies carved out by politicians' ambition and skullduggery.

These puzzle pieces often reach reporters as leaks—information given to the press with its source hidden from the public. Leaks come in many varieties, including the "vendetta leak" designed to damage a political enemy and the "inoculation leak" that is used to release bad news with the most favorable spin on it.

Professional politicians develop sophisticated leaking techniques as they try to influence public opinion. Hedrick Smith, in his book *The Power Game*, described the phenomenon this way: "On Wall Street, passing inside information to others is an indictable offense. In Washington, it is the regular stuff of the power game. Everyone does it, from presidents on down, when they want to change the balance of power on some issue."[24]

Alexander Haig, secretary of state during the early years of the Reagan administration, said that leaks "were a way of governing." As a planned element of the Reagan staff's ongoing public relations efforts, said Haig, "leaks constituted policy; they were the authentic voice of government."[25] By leaking selected information, White House staff members sought subtly to dictate the content of news reports.

This tactic often works because many journalists find leaks irresistible. Whispered bits of information are made more appealing when prefaced by the warning "Look, don't tell anyone I told you this. . . ."

Passing on that information to the public is usually fine. Leaked material may turn out to be "the bits of string that, when pulled, frequently enable reporters to unravel the fabric of hidden scandal."[26]

Reporters, however, should beware of being used inappropriately. Leakers know that when their information is given the imprimatur of a respected news organization, it becomes "news," not mere gossip. Learning the leaker's true motive may be impossible, but usually altruism can be ruled out. Particular care should be exercised when the leaked material is damaging to someone else. The press should not do political operatives' dirty work for them.

For example, in 1988, a tip that Senator Joe Biden had plagiarized speeches turned into a major story, leading to his withdrawal from the Democratic presidential race. The leak had come from John Sasso, top aide to Michael Dukakis, one of Biden's rivals. This, too, was deemed newsworthy, so follow-up stories named Sasso as the source. Dukakis hadn't been told what was going on, and was furious. Sasso resigned.

Jody Powell, who was President Jimmy Carter's press secretary, claims that during the 1980 presidential campaign, Ronald Reagan's advisers regularly leaked information designed to embarrass Carter. "In most cases," wrote Powell, "journalists were too smart to be taken in, but not always. In a few instances, they seemed to be disinclined to risk ruining a good story by checking it too closely."[27]

Gamesmanship in leaking can become complex. Consider this example of the "double-whammy" leak: During the 1988 race for the Republican presidential nomination, supporters of Jack Kemp leaked damaging allegations about George Bush's purported extramarital affairs. The primary target was Bush. But the Kemp backers also were out to damage yet another contender, Bob Dole. So when making the charges about Bush, the leakers (Kemp people) claimed they were Dole supporters. Ideally, news reports would paint Bush as an unfaithful husband and Dole as the slimy source of the rumors.[28]

Sometimes original sources of leaks hide behind one or more intermediaries. For instance, Source A wants to get a story to Reporter B, but doesn't want it known that it came from him (A). So A finds out that B will soon be interviewing politician C. C's top aide, D, is a friend of A. So A gives the information to D, who passes it on to C, who leaks it—on condition of anonymity, of course—to B, who puts it in the paper. For A, mission accomplished: the leak is published and his or her tracks are covered.

If this seems convoluted, that's because it is. It's the kind of maneuvering reporters must contend with. To get the whole story, they must travel hard-to-follow trails to find the ultimate source of a leak.

Because that's often impossible, journalists are better off using leaked information as merely a lead that might take them to on-the-record sources. The ethical obligation remains accuracy, and if a reporter is not reasonably certain that leaked information is true, the best course is to withhold it from the public until it has been corroborated.

Even when sources are willing to eschew coy leaking and go on the record, a reporter must make judgments about the quality of the material being provided. Although it's attributed, something that's wrong is still wrong. And if it's published, the news consumer is getting bad information. A correction after the fact probably won't be seen by all those who saw the initial report.

So part of a reporter's job is to evaluate sources, particularly those who might be relied on frequently. Judgments are based partly on track record, partly on instinct.

During a presidential campaign, for instance, reporters will have only limited access to the candidate, so the candidate's staff becomes an essential conduit of information. This might seem to be a logical, simple flow, but that's not always the case.

When the quality of information depends on the quality of a secondhand source (as opposed to material the reporter can gather firsthand, from the primary source), strict criteria must be used in judging reliability. Willingness to talk to the press does not, in itself, mean the source is a good one. Here are some questions that reporters might ask themselves:

— Is the source knowledgeable? Not everyone working for a campaign knows what's going on in that campaign. As in most organizations, the campaign staff contains an elite that understands goals and strategies, and generally provides the most accurate information. Plenty of other campaign workers, even honest and well-intentioned ones, may pass on bad information, thinking it's accurate.

— Does the source really speak for the candidate? Sometimes a campaign staff member's views are more his or her own than those of the candidate. The public wants the latter, not the former. Reporters, therefore, must evaluate sources' relationships to their boss. Jody Powell, Jimmy Carter's press secretary, and George Stephanopoulos, director of communications for Bill Clinton, were known to be very close to those presidents and could be trusted to be truly speaking for them when they said they were. If Stephanopoulos, for example, told a reporter that Clinton had changed his mind about allowing Haitian refugees into the country, that would be just about as good as hearing it from the president himself. The journalist could go with the story (including attributing the statement to Stephanopoulos). On the other hand, if an assistant press secretary or someone else "farther down the food chain" made the same claim, the reporter should seek further corroboration.

— Is the source trustworthy? Like all politicians, sources play games, often of Byzantine complexity, and have no hesitancy about using the news media as pawns. Motives vary. Sources may be trying to advance their own careers by leaking information flattering to themselves, regardless of its accuracy. Or they may want to embarrass a rival within the campaign staff by blaming a foul-up on that adversary. The list is as extensive as politicians' ambitions—virtually endless.

From the office seeker's perspective, relationships between staff and individual reporters are important because they influence the collective news media's—and thus the public's—perception of the candidate. The relationship isn't always happy. Reporters can develop intense dislike of staff members for reasons such as untruthfulness and inefficiency. (A rule for campaign staff: Never lie to reporters or lose their luggage.)

This was one of the many aspects of press relations that Richard Nixon never understood. For instance, Nixon's press secretary, Ron Ziegler, was described as "smug, condescending, and relentlessly evasive, often refusing to answer the simplest and most innocuous of questions."[29] In theory, objective journalists will ignore such abuse when they write their stories, but they're unlikely to forget it altogether. The cumulative effect of such treatment is a poisoned relationship between press and candidate. In Nixon's case, this mutual antipathy certainly exacerbated his problems during numerous policy crises and especially during the Watergate scandal.

Evaluating sources goes hand in hand with cultivating them. Journalists always want one more source; they're forever on the lookout for people who might have that last piece missing from the puzzle. Even if that source might be needed only once in a journalist's career, his or her name and phone number are worth having.

Of course, no potential source *has* to talk to a reporter. Public spirit or self-interest might motivate them to do so, but often the journalist has to spend considerable time making a case so the person with information will talk.

This leads back to the "friend or adversary" debate. Relationships with sources usually are different from those with actual subjects of coverage. A conflict of interest may be less likely. The reporter's portrayal of a source probably won't be influenced by their personal relationship, and even if it is, it probably will be of less consequence. For most stories, news consumers care little about the source's motivation and credentials; they're interested in getting good information.

Nevertheless, journalists shouldn't let down their guard altogether. Many sources have their own, far from altruistic agendas that they are eager to push. Sometimes these are personal, sometimes they advance the cause of the source's boss. Whatever the purpose behind this advocacy, reporters should carefully protect news channels to the public.

When reporters schmooze with presidential campaign aides late at night in a hotel bar in Iowa, New Hampshire, or one of the other stops along the campaign trail, they remain agents of the public. Bonds tend to develop after hours, when the entire campaign entourage seeks to escape pressures of the daily grind. Those ties can help information-gathering or they can color coverage. Distinctions between the two are often fuzzy.

So, like contacts with the candidates or officeholders themselves, the arms-length relationship should be preserved in dealing with the staff. For one thing, if the candidate wins, members of his or her campaign staff may assume government positions that deserve coverage. Today's campaign gofer may be on tomorrow's national Security Council staff. Because the unelected government tends not to get the scrutiny it should, groundwork for this potential coverage should be laid during the campaign.

In all these cases, journalists will benefit from heeding this axiom: If you want a friend, get a dog.

PUBLIC PERCEPTIONS

News consumers' perceptions of the relationship between journalists and politicians help shape their judgments about the quality and honesty of news coverage. If they believe this relationship is too close, they are likely to trust reporters just about as much as they trust politicians. From the journalists' standpoint, that's terrible.

As with other cases of conflicts of interest, perception can be as weighty as reality is. Even if no actual conflict exists, it might just as well, if news consumers think it does.

Public suspicion of the news media follows different courses, depending on the prevalent mood of the moment. Sometimes the press is disliked because it is a provocative outsider; it seems to be a destructive army arrayed against a popular political figure. For instance, even Richard Nixon was immensely popular at one time—he carried forty-nine states in the 1972 election—and he pilloried journalists for undermining his presidency.

On the other hand, the press corps sometimes angers voters because it seems too much the insider, conspiring with the powers that be to rig the political game. An unconventional candidate such as Ross Perot can make that kind of charge.

The only thing journalists know for certain is that someone will always be finding fault with them. Disparate public values make particularly important the need for care in defining limits of propriety when gathering news from subjects and sources.

Reporters might say, "We're just doing our jobs, and we can't help what the public thinks about us." That's too facile a response. A credible press— and for that matter, a free press—depends on public faith, if not always absolute public approval.

Swirling currents of public sentiment took quantitative form in an opinion poll done shortly after a televised confrontation between CBS anchorman Dan Rather and Vice President George Bush. The setting: a live interview on "The CBS Evening News" following a tough, extensive package about Bush's alleged involvement in the Iran-Contra scandal. The time: the early stages of the 1988 presidential campaign, when Bush's quest for the Republican nomination seemed in jeopardy, in part because the candidate was having trouble shaking the image of being a "wimp."

Bush, who said he'd expected the package to be a more general campaign profile, angrily charged that he'd been set up. Rather pushed hard, trying to get Bush to explain apparent contradictions in his statements about Iran-Contra matters.

Rather: I don't want to be argumentative, Mr. Vice President.

Bush: You do, Dan.

The battle raged for nine minutes and ended with little new information revealed about the scandal, but with lots of very visible ill will between two men at the tops of their respective professions.

Resuming his campaigning, Bush declared himself the victor in the face-off, a courageous St. George slaying the news media dragon. Rather defended his role, taking time on the next evening's newscast to say, "Trying to ask honest questions and trying to be persistent about answers is part of a reporter's job."

A survey conducted by Yankelovich Clancy Shulman for *Time* magazine elicited mixed public opinions. Asked "Who came out ahead in the exchange?" 42 percent of respondents said Bush, 27 percent said Rather. In answer, however, to "Whom do you trust more to tell the truth?" 22 percent said Bush, while 49 percent said Rather.

When asked "Do you think Rather was rude to Bush in the interview?" "Yes" prevailed, 51 to 38 percent. But in answer to "Was Rather right to push Bush on his role in the Iran-Contra affair?" 59 percent said "Yes," to 32 percent "No."[30]

The responses to these last two questions illustrate the ambivalence running through public attitudes about the news media. People don't like a journalist being rude or arrogant, but they understand the need for aggressive reporting. The public isn't stupid; politicians'—and the truth's—slipperiness is recognized.

Several lessons emerge from this case. First, journalists should be aware that the public is judging their behavior as they gather the news. Second, this concern about tactics does not necessarily supersede interest in the quality of the ultimate news product.

For journalists, this is yet another ethical tightrope that must be walked.

"HORSE RACE JOURNALISM"

"You people cover campaigns as if they were horse races" is a frequently heard criticism about political journalism. In many cases, it's right on target.

The analogy is irresistible, and often apt. "Coming into the home stretch, it's Clinton with the lead . . . Bush is running his heart out and closing the gap . . . and on the outside, here comes Perot!" Drop the racetrack vernacular and you have a standard news account of the 1992 presidential contest's final days.

Using reportorial aids ranging from polls to intuition, journalists devote much effort to telling news consumers who's ahead in a campaign. Of course, the premise is flawed in the sense that only on Election Day, after ballots are cast, do any substantive grounds exist for ranking winners and losers. Anything earlier is merely speculation—scientific or otherwise—about what *might* happen.

In itself, this is basically harmless, introducing a sense of sportlike competition to enliven coverage on those many days when little of import is happening. And the public does get interested in who will win.

But horse race journalism can have two significant negative impacts:

— The thrill of the race may become so heavily emphasized that stories about issues and other complex matters get pushed aside.

— Journalists may become more touts than reporters, developing a proprietary interest in seeing their predictions prove correct. If one of the horses becomes *their* horse, coverage may subtly start enhancing that horse's prospects.

Of course, the ability to win an election is not unlike the ability to govern. For good or ill, American government is the domain of politicians, not philosophers. A successful campaigner must demonstrate the ability to organize, to persuade, and to lead, all of which are essential in successful governing. So news coverage of these skills is useful in giving voters a complete picture of their choices.

Also, the structure of the electoral process is similar to a sport's season. A presidential campaign, for instance, has its starting gate or opening day—the Iowa caucuses. After a months-long contest it has its finish line or Super Bowl—Election Day. The politicians—not the press—devised this calendar.

Accurate reporting requires some horse race judgments by the press corps. Coverage cannot—and should not—be universal. As Election Day draws near, some offices will be sought by dozens of candidates, many of whom will have negligible support. In making horse race evaluations, reporters are telling voters, "Look, these are the candidates we think have realistic chances to win; these are the ones whose qualifications you should examine most closely."

Maybe a political campaign *is* a horse race. But even horse races merit ethical coverage.

THE SCREENING PROCESS

Planning political coverage—especially during the early stages of a campaign—requires meeting some daunting mathematical challenges.

News organizations' staffs and bankrolls are limited, making coverage of large numbers of candidates unfeasible. Fortunately, few contests are as overwhelming as the 1961 Texas special election to fill the U.S. Senate seat vacated when Lyndon Johnson became vice president. In that campaign, seventy-one candidates were on the ballot.

More common are situations such as that seen in the 1992 presidential campaign. The Republican field was small; George Bush and Pat Buchanan were the only major candidates. Democrats, however, had a wider choice: Bill Clinton, Paul Tsongas, Jerry Brown, Tom Harkin, and Bob Kerrey all had to be taken seriously as the race began.

But newsroom economics and journalistic formats won't allow perfectly evenhanded coverage. For example, if you're a network newscast producer and you want to run a story about the upcoming New Hampshire primary, must you include every candidate in the report?

Of course not. If you tried to do so, you'd end up filling your entire show with politics. The vast majority of viewers won't stand for that.

So decisions must be made. During any given week, you might be able to spread the coverage around. If the five leading Democrats are all campaigning within the limited confines of Iowa or New Hampshire, the mechanics of reporting their activities aren't too difficult. (You'll probably have every candidate come up to shake your hand if you just station yourself on a street corner in Manchester, New Hampshire, during primary season.)

At some point, however, political coverage planners must decide who merits everyday reports; who should be accompanied on cross-country campaign trips; who should be presented to the public as having a reasonable chance of becoming the next president.

That kind of coverage will not be accorded even to all major contenders, and certainly not to so-called minor candidates (discussed below). Even before voters make their choices, the field must be narrowed. This is the screening process. It is fraught with ethical problems.

Decisions about whom to cover are rarely based on ideological or personal favoritism. Rather, the criteria are grounded in pragmatism. Candidates are evaluated on the basis of the professionalism of their campaign organizations and the size of their campaign treasuries. Added to this are poll results plus reporters' experience-based judgments about campaigns' relative viability.

From this process emerge decisions about who are front-runners and who are also-rans. These labels can be exceptionally important. Front-runners get coverage that assures them full consideration by voters, especially those most important voters who might become financial contributors and campaign volunteers. Those considered also-rans face the "out of sight, out of mind" problem and a disastrous Catch-22: if they don't get coverage, they won't get public support (in polls and contributions); and if they don't get that support, they won't get coverage.

Candidates are rightly sensitive about this. For example, in 1980, John Connally mounted a major presidential campaign, spending $12 million to contest Ronald Reagan, George Bush, and others for the Republican nomination. A few months into the race, he was preparing to drop out. He complained bitterly that the press "wrote my obituary long ago," not by saying bad things but by saying relatively nothing at all about him. While Reagan's and Bush's doings were the daily stuff of page 1, Connally's campaign was written about on page 25, and even there only sporadically. No candidate can survive that for long.

This was partly Connally's own fault. His campaign strategy was fatally flawed; he delayed his major push on the assumption that Reagan would falter early. Although few delegates had been chosen by the time of Connally's targeted primaries, the screening process had by then narrowed the field to Reagan and Bush.

Screening is not done by some secretive cabal eager to control the political system. No formal "screening committee" exists. The process is driven by informal gossip and journalists reading, seeing, or hearing their colleagues' work. Conventional wisdom develops (based on the criteria mentioned above) and takes hold. As editors and producers subscribe to it, the journalistic pack's coverage gravitates to it.

Sometimes a candidate survives despite being screened out of front-runner ranks. In the 1984 presidential campaign, for instance, the press declared Walter Mondale and John Glenn to be leading the pack. A combination of Gary Hart's good grass-roots organization, Glenn's ineptitude, and Mondale's overconfidence helped Hart pull off a smashing upset win in the New Hampshire primary. Voters in effect vetoed the screening decision.

That happens rarely. Screening creates an implicit pronouncement by the news media: "Here are the only candidates worthy of your consideration." Many voters have neither the time nor the inclination to challenge that by checking out candidates on their own.

Screening thus subverts voters' freedom of choice and narrows the field of issues as well as of candidates. Take, for example, the 1992 presidential candidacy of Larry Agran. He was no kook; he was a Harvard Law School graduate and former mayor of Irvine, California, with some interesting ideas, particularly about urban issues. Despite being well received by voters and some other politicians at a number of candidate forums, most of the national press corps ignored him.

Occasionally some coverage slipped through. The *New York Times* reported about a U.S. Conference of Mayors session where "dozens of mayors . . . seemed to agree on one thing: the single candidate who truly understands urban needs is Larry Agran."[31] This, however, was an isolated report. The television networks still considered him a nonperson.

Based on the standard criteria of money, organization, campaign apparatus, public recognition, and so forth, Agran was a sure loser. And that evaluation—logical as it may seem, given the prevalent rules of the game—precluded voters from hearing what Agran had to say. *Washington Post* columnist Colman McCarthy was one of the few journalists championing Agran's right to be heard—specifically, calling for including Agran in televised debates among Democratic presidential hopefuls. According to McCarthy, "A major abuse in the media is not that we slant the news, but that we can arbitrarily choose the news. The Agran blackout exemplifies that this is a journalistic crime easily gotten away with."[32]

According to the noted philosopher Yogi Berra, "It ain't over 'til it's over." But for some candidates and many voters, the screening process means the campaign is over even before it really begins.

Such condescension by the press toward voters—"We'll make your choices for you"—goes beyond ethical bounds. Fairness requires that voters have the opportunity to consider the full spectrum of candidates and issues.

But not all the responsibility for this should fall on the news media. The public must do some work, too. For instance, even if TV covers the Larry Agrans of politics, it certainly will do so only briefly. That's an inescapable function of the TV news format. So voters must read the newspapers and magazines that can present deeper coverage. Nothing is unethical about the press sharing responsibility with the public.

EXPECTATIONS

Reporter: How well do you hope to do in tomorrow's primary?
Candidate: Better than expected.

In much the same way they orchestrate the screening process, the news media define electoral victory and defeat. If this were merely a matter of arithmetic, whoever garnered the most votes would be the winner and everyone else would be the losers. But politics isn't that logical.

Particularly in the early primaries, candidates run not only against other politicians but also against expectations. For the dark horse, a second-place finish can be a victory. And for a front-runner, first place without a comfortable margin may be a defeat. All this depends on meeting, failing to meet, or exceeding expectations.

For example, as the 1972 presidential campaign began, Senator Edmund Muskie of Maine was the odds-on favorite to win the Democratic nomination. Expectations were high that he would get off to a great start with a solid primary victory in neighboring New Hampshire. To journalists covering the race, getting 60 percent of the vote—and certainly at least half—seemed a reasonable expectation.

But Muskie ended up with 46 percent, while South Dakota Senator George McGovern—who had already been labeled an also-ran—won 37 percent. Despite the math, Muskie was judged by many journalists and politicians to be the loser, and McGovern the winner. The front-runner suddenly looked vulnerable, and the dark horse had become a viable contender.

That case underscores the potential dangers and benefits of the expectations game. In the early stages of a campaign, when candidacies are fragile, potential endorsers and contributors are evaluating the field, keeping in mind the old political adage, "Don't back no losers."

For a candidate, the ideal position is to be a well-placed underdog with an efficient but unobtrusive campaign. "You built your strength quietly, surprised the press in an early caucus or primary in Iowa or New Hampshire, and then sat back and reaped the publicity bonanza."[33] In three successive presidential election years—1976, 1980, and 1984—Jimmy Carter, George Bush, and Gary Hart played this role well. (Sustaining the campaign is another matter; of these three, only Carter went on to win the nomination that year.)

Because the stakes are so high and because expectations tend to be taken seriously by many voters as well as by political insiders, expectations should be devised with care by journalists. To do otherwise is to intrude improperly. Once again, the line between covering and participating should not be crossed.

Expectation-setting relies on many of the same criteria used in the screening process. Added to the mix are the candidate's own expectations. Most experienced politicians are skilled at lowballing. They try to convince journalists that they'll do poorly, so they can more easily reach the better-than-expected plateau. The press corps, of course, knows the pols are doing this.

Occasionally, a candidate or campaign staff member will be foolish enough to state an unrealistically high expectation. Journalists generally will shrug and say "Fine," and then they'll hang that prognostication around the candidate's neck.

All this has a certain childishness about it. A politician's doing better or worse than expected can provide insight about a candidacy's prospects. But turning this into a predictions game doesn't do much to help the public decide who should hold office.

Ethical problems arise when reporters use expectations to trip a front-runner in order to make the campaign more interesting. This is like a high-jumping competition in which the bar is raised after every successful jump. Eventually—inevitably—it will reach a height at which it can't be cleared. So setting expectations should be guided by a standard of reasonableness.

Also, journalists certainly should not have such a stake in setting expectations that their treatment of a candidate is keyed to whether those expectations are met. For example, in 1980, George Bush exceeded expectations and was quickly proclaimed the front-runner by many journalists when he upset Ronald Reagan in the Iowa caucuses. Expectations for Bush then soared; he became the media's anointed "man to beat," gracing news magazine covers and being otherwise celebrated. Then reality reasserted itself; Reagan got his campaign on track and soundly beat Bush in the New Hampshire primary. Some journalists reacted as if they were jilted lovers. "Their" George Bush had failed to meet their expectations. Perhaps partly due to this, the tone of some Bush coverage switched from awestruck to sour.

Similarly, Election Night analysis of primary or caucus returns should keep the expectations issue in perspective. It's largely an artificial standard. Although meeting or failing to meet expectations can affect a candidacy's momentum (which may be another illusory force), this is rarely a determinative factor in a long campaign.

Another example involving George Bush: In 1988, much to-do was made about religious broadcaster Pat Robertson's second-place showing in the Iowa caucuses, behind Bob Dole and ahead of Bush. Certainly Robertson had exceeded expectations, just as Bush had failed to meet them. But as the campaign progressed, this showing proved to be a fluke. Bush rebounded; Robertson faded. The Iowa performance vis-à-vis expectations turned out to mean virtually nothing. Journalists who overrated the importance of this vote did their audience a disservice.

MAINTAINING PERSPECTIVE

On the road, a presidential campaign can become a truly insular enterprise, politicians and press wrapped together like astronauts in a spaceship's tight cocoon.

The real world intrudes only sporadically, seen whizzing past the windows of a police-escorted motorcade bus. Sometimes the people along the streets are applauding, but often they seem merely mystified. They hadn't been told that the circus was coming to town, and now that it's here, they don't care.

Even most of the "civilians" the press corps sees are denizens of the political periphery—the faithful who jam themselves into spotlight-drenched auditoriums and dutifully cheer the candidate's well-worn applause lines.

After the day's official events are over, the spaceship's crew—pols and journalists—remains intact, eating, drinking, and sometimes sleeping together.

Aside from the dangers of bias and conflict of interest that can accompany such personal closeness, life on the road can affect reportorial judgment and accuracy. For instance, in *The Boys on the Bus*, Tim Crouse tells of reporters—smart, experienced reporters—traveling with the McGovern campaign who believed near the end of the race that McGovern was going to win.[34] He ended up winning Massachusetts and the District of Columbia, while Richard Nixon swept the rest of the country.

These reporters' misjudgment was only partly a manifestation of anti-Nixon wishful thinking. Primarily it was the product of tunnel vision caused by too many hours in the campaign spaceship's rarefied atmosphere. If, for example, you're traveling with the McGovern entourage, you go to McGovern rallies, you see crowds cheering McGovern, you talk to McGovern staff members. Everything is upbeat. All that you're seeing is real, but it's a very narrow slice of reality.

Journalists must report accurately, so breadth of vision is crucial. That means making a conscious effort to break out of the bubble. Simply escaping the physical and psychological confines of the campaign for a few hours can help. So can talking with some "real people"—those whose lives don't revolve around politics.

Political journalism often seems irrelevant to many news consumers. That's partly due to reporters becoming too much the insiders. Somewhere a line exists—its precise location is hard to define—between getting far enough inside a campaign to glean the best information, and getting so far inside that loyalties and judgments may suffer. Finding and heeding that line are important ethical tasks.

Another problem arising when journalists get caught up in the frantic pace of day-to-day campaigning is missing important "big picture" stories. For example, in 1988, Democratic nominee Michael Dukakis fell from a lead in midsummer polls of fifteen-plus points to an eight-point defeat on Election Day. That collapse didn't happen overnight, but this story was as underreported as it was intriguing. Sure, plenty of reports were printed or aired daily about Dukakis's stumbles and Bush's successful attacks, but the larger context was mostly ignored until the campaign ended.

That kind of story should be covered. Journalists should recognize that doing so requires not letting daily campaign pressures blot out broader perspective.

COVERING UNUSUAL CANDIDACIES

The press corps is part of the presidential campaign establishment. Journalists understand and are comfortable with the traditional party-dominated processes—delegate selection, conventions, debates, advertising, media events, and so on. When election year rolls around, the political press corps revs up its coverage machinery and cranks out journalism that in many respects isn't much different from that produced four years before.

Sometimes, however, the system is knocked askew by extraordinary events or atypical candidates. Their presence requires revising coverage schemes. But the news media—like other institutions—get comfortable with the status quo and don't always respond well to change. Quality of coverage suffers, and news consumers receive an inferior product.

The candidacies of Jesse Jackson in 1984 and 1988, and of Ross Perot in 1992 (and beyond), tested journalists. Results were mixed at best.

Jackson's 1984 candidacy presented news organizations with several ethical questions. First, should he be covered as a serious presidential candidate, like Mondale, Hart, and others? Based on a hardheaded analysis of his chances of winning the White House, at least that year, the answer had to be "No." Despite his high name recognition, he didn't have the organization or money for the sophisticated campaign that presidential politics requires. Also, polls indicated very limited appeal beyond his African-American base. Probably no reporter for a major news organization believed that Jackson would win the presidency, or even the Democratic nomination, in 1984.

On the other hand, almost all those same reporters would agree that the Jackson candidacy was historically important. No other black American had captured such public interest as a national candidate. He was helping shape the year's issues agenda by forcefully championing the interests of those Americans whose concerns rarely got much attention from the powers that be.

So he wasn't going to win, but he had to be covered. For reporters traveling with Jackson, this raised the further question of how tough the coverage should be. Should his every issue position be subject to the same scrutiny as Mondale's proposals, or should he be treated more as historic celebrity than as potential officeholder? And if the later course were to be chosen, would that be patronizing to the point of being racist?

Race was an inescapable element in covering Jackson. For example, Jackson complained that news reporting lapsed into stereotyping that impaired his ability to win white support.

The news media says every night, "Jesse Jackson, black leader." It never says, "Walter Mondale, white leader. Gary Hart, white leader." The reinforcement of the blackness almost makes whites feel excluded, unwelcome, and that's a double standard. I mean, why should the media keep referring to me as a black leader? My blackness is self-evident.[35]

His point is well taken. If black candidates (for president or any other office) do not aim their campaigns only at black voters and do not address issues solely in race-related contexts, their race should not be constantly portrayed as the principal characteristic of their candidacies.

Another issue about covering Jackson was who should do it. If reporters were assigned to the Jackson campaign regardless of their race, news organizations might claim that this proved they were above racism. But a counterargument could be made: "If Jackson appealed, by intention, primarily to blacks, could white reporters adequately appreciate the nuances and contexts of his rhetoric, and would they have the contacts needed to judge whether his pitch was being well received?"[36]

To complicate this further, questions arise from the journalists' standpoint. Do black reporters owe Jackson special loyalty? Should they protect him against an intrinsically racist white media establishment?

Early in the 1984 campaign, this became an explosive issue when Jackson, in conversation with *Washington Post* reporter Milton Coleman, referred to Jews as "Hymies" and to New York City as "Hymietown." A presidential candidate's use of such slurs is clearly newsworthy. But when Coleman, who is black, was identified as the source of the quotes (which appeared in another *Post* reporter's story), he was accused by some blacks of having betrayed Jackson. Nation of Islam leader Louis Farrakhan threatened "to punish [Coleman] with death." Tensions between black and white reporters covering Jackson grew until Jackson helped calm them by pointing out that "there's a dynamic going on that hasn't gone on before . . . we're all going through changes."[37]

Jackson's 1984 candidacy illustrated that the criteria of the screening process can be altered for at least two reasons: if journalists believe that the special nature of a campaign—in this case a historic run by a minority candidate—is in itself worthy of coverage; and if the public is interested in the personality or issues involved. Ability to win the White House may be given little weight.

By 1988 and Jackson's second run for the presidency, the press had grown more accustomed to his presence on the national scene and had developed a better sense of how to treat his candidacy.

For one thing, Jackson eventually came to be taken far more seriously. At the campaign's outset, reporters tended to underestimate his ability to win white votes, but that changed as his showings improved. In March, for example, Jackson won 25 percent of the vote in the Texas primary, finishing second behind Michael Dukakis, and won the Michigan caucuses with 55 percent of the turnout.

Such vote-getting performance elevated Jackson into the ranks of "serious candidates," which meant that coverage became more serious. For instance, shortly after his Michigan triumph, *The New Republic*'s Fred Barnes wrote a tough analysis of Jackson's standard stump speech, which Barnes said was filled with inaccuracies.[38] Until then, Jackson's vaguely defined "special" status had largely exempted him from such scrutiny.

Jackson's candidacy forced journalists to come to grips with issues such as race and allocation of coverage. If one main ethical lesson is to be found in this, it is that broadening coverage—and doing so seriously, not conde-scendingly—will give news consumers a far more accurate picture of political reality.

In 1992, another "special candidacy" challenged news organizations' standard operating procedures. Texas billionaire Ross Perot flaunted his disdain for the news media. "The reporters' unspoken threat—if you don't answer our questions, we won't put you on TV—is meaningless to a candidate who can buy all the airtime he wants, whenever he wants."[39]

Perot's sudden emergence on the political scene sent journalists scram-bling to define who he is and what he stands for. He had painstakingly cultivated his image as an iconoclastic defender of common sense. That "billionaire populist" might be an oxymoron bothered him not at all.

His money and notoriety ensured Perot a place in the campaign spot-light. By skillfully using talk shows such as "Larry King Live," he could reach millions of voters without subjecting himself to tough questioning from reporters. Opinion polls showed his popularity soaring; by late spring he led both Bush and Clinton in some surveys.

So the news media couldn't simply dismiss this outsider, but they also couldn't force him to play by the unwritten rules that ensure at least some accountability of candidates to press and public. Perot made it clear he would talk to reporters only when and if he chose to do so. Other than trips to television studios for talk shows or taping ads, he spent most of his time out of sight, venturing out to only a few public rallies.

Reporters had to work with whatever information they could find. Perot's business practices—some of which were ethically questionable— were scrutinized. His aphorisms about economics and the state of the country had been collected and were available for analysis. He had feuded with some politicians—most notably George Bush—and that provided grist for the journalistic mill.

Perot's presence certainly enlivened the presidential race, raising plenty of questions about the relevance of the existing party structure and the potential impact of independent candidacies on the electoral college sys-tem. He quickly galvanized a massive grass-roots base, as volunteers mounted extraordinarily successful petition drives to put him on the ballot around the country. He hired some top professional political operatives, dropped out of the race (which he had never formally entered) in July, and then reemerged as a declared candidate in October, just in time to be invited to join Bush and Clinton in a series of televised debates.

The challenge of covering Perot was made more difficult by the way Clinton and Bush treated their opponent. Both hoped that large numbers of Perot backers would return to the conventional fold on Election Day and support one of them. So neither the president nor his Democratic challenger wanted to alienate this potentially decisive voter bloc. They rarely criticized Perot, and when they did so, they proceeded gingerly.

This deprived reporters of a staple of the campaign feeding frenzy—the blood spilled during attack and counterattack. A few allegations about Perot may have been leaked by the Bush and Clinton camps, but reporters were mostly left to their own devices. Some stories emerged, mainly focusing on what seemed to be Perot's occasionally odd behavior—his response to a purported Republican plot to disrupt his daughter's wedding, his claims of having repelled a team of assassins from his front lawn, and so forth.

Such stories appeared during the campaign's final weeks, accompanied by Perot's denunciations of reporters for sullying his character. But patchwork coverage never produced a coherent portrait of this man who would be president. Voters went to the polls on November 3 knowing less than they should have about Ross Perot.

Although covering Perot was challenging, journalists' ethical obligations were the same as in reporting about Clinton and Bush. Even if the candidate tried to hide behind his wall of money by using half-hour commercials to paint his self-portrait, news organizations should have been more aggressive. His business and personal background could have been more thoroughly examined. His platform could have been more carefully scrutinized. And his overall fitness to be president could have been more thoughtfully analyzed.

For the press, the principal ethical lesson emerging from the 1992 Perot campaign was that candidates should not be allowed to define unilaterally how they are to be covered. The news media, as the public's surrogates, must not let themselves be pushed around or distracted. Particularly with wealthy candidates, news organizations should beware of efforts to circumvent traditional news channels by relying almost exclusively on purchased and controlled media vehicles.

Ross Perot spent at least $63 million of his own money and won more than 19 million votes. Both those numbers should inspire journalists to think carefully about what they did in 1992 and what they will do about similar candidacies in the future.

COVERING POLITICAL INSTITUTIONS

Coverage tends to gravitate toward people and events. Stories about the candidate or rally, or an update about the horse race, can be told simply and are likely to be understood by even the news consumer with limited knowledge of politics. Television journalists particularly like these topics because much of the story can be told in pictures.

Sometimes, however, more important news is to be found in the far less glamorous institutions of politics. For example, in 1972, George McGovern's unexpected emergence as presidential nominee didn't happen just because of McGovern's personal qualities or even because of his issues positions. The key to his success was the reform of Democratic Party nominating procedures that had taken place after the disastrous 1968 national convention in Chicago. Becoming a convention delegate was made more a function of grass-roots organizing than of old-boy-network connections. Antiwar activists supporting McGovern did the best job of taking advantage of these changes. Not coincidentally, the chair of the delegate selection reform committee had been George McGovern.

This was a big story, but it went largely unreported until after McGovern's nomination. Even McGovern staff members remarked on the press's lack of understanding of the nominating process.[40] One reason for this oversight was that the reform procedures were complicated and many participants were unknown except to a few political insiders.

A more recent institutional change that also received too little attention was the Democratic Party's move toward the ideological center after losing five of six presidential elections, beginning in 1968. One of the early champions of pragmatic centrism was Arkansas Governor Bill Clinton. When he became a presidential nominee in 1992, his decidedly nonliberal stance on issues such as capital punishment made Democrats much less vulnerable to the usual attacks from Republicans about being too far to the left to represent the great moderate middle of the American electorate.

Doing these stories would have required focusing on the party per se. But a party doesn't have a face, and structural and ideological reforms are incremental. Dramatic party events that lend themselves to terse coverage are few and far between.

According to the conventional wisdom accepted by many journalists, complexity scares off news consumers, so many reporters veer away from covering complicated matters. (Also, although most journalists won't admit it, reporting about complex topics requires lots of work, another disincentive.)

Avoiding stories about political institutions is bad journalism on two counts: it lets important stories go unreported and, by assuming the voters want their news only in nuggets, it's patronizing toward them.

Ethical journalism requires presenting the whole story—or at least as much of the story as is reasonably available—to news consumers.

Put simply, shortchanging the public is unethical.

For journalists on the bus, life is a mix of adrenalin rushes and exhaustion, of being cogs in electoral machinery and being parts of history.

It's an important job, an essential element in the making of presidents and other officeholders. These journalists bouncing along on planes and trains and buses wield great power. Ethical journalism requires that they recognize this and wield it thoughtfully.

Chapter Five

Campaign Advertising

Politicians communicate with voters through two principal vehicles: free media, meaning news coverage, and paid media, which includes advertising, direct mail, telephone banks, and other mechanisms the candidate controls.

In a politician's perfect world, free media's content would be limited to news reports of daily campaign events, with just an occasional annoying story about records and issues. (Of course, negative stories about an opponent are always fine.) The candidate's paid media would tell the voters what they really need to know and would be outside the scope of press scrutiny.

Although politicians might be well served by such limits on news coverage, voters would be shortchanged. Many candidates count heavily on paid media to win votes, so their messages should not go unexamined. For example, Ross Perot in 1992 did his best to circumvent news coverage, keeping public appearances and contact with reporters to a minimum while using his vast personal wealth to flood television airwaves with advertising. Perot's money let him rely on ads far more than most candidates can, but his use of this medium is instructive nevertheless. If they had the bankroll, many other candidates would do the same thing.

ADVERTISING'S IMPACT

Voters use disparate sources of information to make their Election Day decisions. A 1992 poll conducted for the Times Mirror Center for the People & the Press found that by a margin of 65 to 18 percent, respondents said they got a better idea of where candidates stand from news reports than from TV commercials. The margin was 63 to 23 percent when asked which source gave them a better idea of what the candidates are like personally.[1]

Clearly, advertising is usually not determinative in itself, but it is influential—certainly influential enough to merit press attention. It not only affects voters' perceptions of candidates' positions and personalities, but also is part of the screening process (which distinguishes front-runners from also-rans), and it helps shape a campaign year's issues agenda.

Understanding the roles that campaign ads play is essential to appreciating the importance of news coverage of those ads. Ads are designed to meet different needs, depending on the campaign calendar and the candidate's position in the race. If, for instance, the campaign is just getting under way and the candidate is little known, the first ads may be designed simply to increase name recognition. Voters won't seriously consider candidates they haven't heard of, so this kind of advertising lets the would-be officeholder get his or her foot in the door, prior to trying the hard sell later in the contest. (Of course, if the field is crowded and these introductory spots don't work, there may be no "later.")

After establishing viability, candidates use ads to convey promises and attack opponents. That's a challenging mission, especially when relying on the standard thirty-second spot. But ads that are cleverly designed and that appear frequently can intrude into voters' consciousness and at least earn the candidate a closer look when he or she is the subject of a news story.

For most offices—those lower on the ballot, with relatively small constituencies—extravagant use of paid media is not cost effective. For example, a city council candidate who insists on running TV ads may reach mostly people who live outside the district. Money spent on those ads would be better used for a precisely targeted mailing.

But for national, statewide, and other offices with large numbers of potential voters, advertising not only is useful, it also is expected of "major" candidates. Ability to advertise is a factor in the screening process (discussed in Chapter 3). Journalists tend to take seriously only those candidates who can play the game fully.

Doing so may just be acknowledging unpleasant reality, considering how money-driven politics is. But journalists should be cautious about precluding the public from considering candidates qualified in every way except wealth, and similarly should be concerned about further equating political merit with political bankroll. The ability to advertise is *not* the same thing as the ability to govern.

Plenty of candidates have used advertising to transform themselves from political unknowns into front-runners. This is most likely to happen during the earliest stages of a campaign. When news coverage is still minimal, advertising's effect is enhanced. Absent objective news reports to counterbalance one-sided ads, candidates can define themselves in the most flattering way. Even though voters always harbor some skepticism about political ads and may be far from making final choices early in the campaign, they are likely to be at least intrigued by candidates who present their messages cleverly.

An example: a wealthy Texas rancher and businessman named Clayton Williams decided he wanted to be elected governor in 1990. His name recognition throughout the state was virtually zero. In 1989, he began running television ads that portrayed him as the quintessential tough-talking cowboy. For instance, he promised that he would introduce drug offenders to "the joys of bustin' rocks." Because of his ample bankroll, production values in the ads were excellent, and plenty of airtime was purchased throughout the state.

These ads transformed Williams from unknown to powerhouse. His primary opponents couldn't match his spending, and he easily won the Republican nomination. In the general election campaign, however, he could not be sustained by ads alone. News coverage, much of it critical, was now in the mix. In the dissonance created by conflicting messages, the ads' impact diminished.

A related issue concerns placement of television political ads. Most stations refuse to run campaign spots during a newscast in order to avoid undercutting credibility of reporting and possibly confusing viewers. Some stations, however, do sell this time to political advertisers, arguing that the news audience is appropriate for these spots and is smart enough to distinguish between news and ads.[2]

Depending on the content of the spot, making that distinction can be difficult. For instance, the 1992 Bush campaign ran ads that looked like the "person on the street" interviews that are frequently used on newscasts. The "average citizens" (in fact, specially recruited Bush supporters) who were intently looking into the camera, all harshly criticized Bill Clinton. When one of these ads appeared in a commercial break directly following a news story about the presidential campaign, the delineation between the two was blurry. Even a sophisticated news consumer who hadn't seen the Bush spot before might well have thought this was a follow-up to the news report.

As a matter of basic fairness both to the news program's audience and to other candidates, extreme caution should be used if ads and news are to be mixed in this way. Clear separation should be established between news and political advertising.

In addition to defining the field of candidates, ads help shape the issues agenda. Campaigners choose issues for their ads based on surveys of voter attitudes. For instance, in a special U.S. Senate election in Texas in 1993, one candidate capitalized on his and his targeted voters' shared opposition to gays being allowed to serve in the military. Whether this was the most pressing issue facing the nation at that time was irrelevant; the candidate thought he could profit from heavy emphasis on that issue, so he used advertising to try to push it to the top of the campaign agenda. (As it turned out, he lost. The strength of his main opponent, not his choice of issues, had the most to do with the outcome.)

Journalists, on the other hand, should make decisions about issue coverage not merely on the basis of voters' "hot button" response but, rather, on independent evaluation of what topics are most germane to the office being sought.

COVERING CAMPAIGN ADS

Journalists should provide counterpoint to campaign advertising. Voters are entitled to facts as well as puffery, to objectivity as well as partisanship. The earlier in a campaign this balance is established, the better.

The question here is who controls a campaign; specifically, how do politicians and journalists share influence? Certainly candidates purchasing advertising have every right to say in their ads whatever they want about whatever issues they want (with some loose constraints, such as about truthfulness of personal attacks on opponents).

But journalists also have the right—and the responsibility—to monitor advertising just as they cover everything else the candidate does. If a candidate's speech to a thousand people merits a news story, so does the candidate's ad that reaches a million people.

Only since 1990 have news organizations shown interest in covering ads consistently. In part, this stemmed from embarrassment about treating the 1988 presidential campaign's TV spots so softly, especially those presented by the Bush campaign. Analyzing the TV networks' performance, Kiku Adatto wrote: "Of the 125 excerpts [of ads] shown on the evening news in 1988, the reporter addressed the veracity of the commercials' claims less than eight percent of the time. The networks became, in effect, electronic billboards for the candidates. . . ."[3]

Media critic Mark Crispin Miller, citing "passive collusion" between the press and Republican media strategists, wrote that coverage of the Bush-Quayle ads left much to be desired:

Typically, each correspondent would address the latest ad with some very obvious comment on the candidate's general tactical intentions. Rarely would he or she do what journalists ought to do with any piece of propaganda: expose its sly half-truths and outright lies, and then correct them.[4]

In 1990, a scattering of newspapers and broadcast stations around the country began assigning reporters to critique the accuracy of promises and attacks in candidates' ads. Bill Monroe wrote in the *Washington Journalism Review*: "For the first time in most places, a referee in the form of a political reporter is showing up in the campaign arena with the savvy to call fouls and a voice that's being heard. A game with a referee is a different kind of game."[5]

By 1992, ads were being covered nationally and locally with far greater frequency. Formats for coverage were developing through trial and error. The "truth testing" process had become much more substantive.

Before examining this kind of reporting, here is some background information about how campaign advertising has influenced American politics. A brief history of this evolution may help establish a context for appraising the ethical significance of covering contemporary candidates' ads.

A BRIEF HISTORY OF CAMPAIGN ADVERTISING

Although TV spots are now the most dominant political ads, American campaign salesmanship dates back to the 18th century. And, as is illustrated in Chapter 3, invective has always influenced—and often dominated—American political discourse. The 1796 battle to succeed George Washington featured broadsides printed by backers of John Adams and Thomas Jefferson. In addition to touting their favorites, these ads disguised as journalism launched a long tradition of trashing the opposition. Adams was reviled as a monarchist and Jefferson as an atheist.

Advertising gambits took various forms in 19th-century campaigning. For example, in the 1840 presidential race, William Henry Harrison, who as a general had won the not particularly consequential battle of Tippecanoe, and whose running mate was the not particularly consequential John Tyler, benefitted from having a nicely alliterative slogan, "Tippecanoe and Tyler, Too." Harrison also was dubbed the "log cabin candidate," and his supporters sometimes were provided with cabin-shaped jugs of whiskey. Such gimmickry helped him defeat the incumbent, Martin Van Buren.

As campaign techniques matured, giveaway items remained popular in building name identification and voter loyalty. During Abraham Lincoln's 1860 campaign, wooden axes and rails allegedly split by the candidate were popular props at rallies and parades. William McKinley's backers in 1896 distributed lapel pins in the shape of a dinner pail, as part of their strategy to win workingmen's support by promising prosperity and "a full dinner pail." In 1904, Theodore Roosevelt benefitted from the popularity of Teddy bears. (This toy's origin was a story that Roosevelt had refused, while on a hunting trip, to shoot a young bear that had been captured for him.)[6]

Meanwhile, newspaper advertising consisted mainly of notices about candidate appearances. News reports focused more on politicians' public utterances (and their alleged peccadilloes) than on their vote-seeking strategies.

The advent of radio did not precipitate an immediate revolution in political advertising. During its first years, radio was seen by candidates as merely a vehicle to deliver the dominant verbal form of campaigning—the formal speech—to a larger audience.[7] Warren Harding was the first president to have his voice beamed overseas by radio, and Calvin Coolidge was the first president to rely heavily on this medium. Coolidge delivered a series of radio speeches in the run-up to the 1924 Republican National Convention.[8]

Coolidge liked the medium.

I am very fortunate that I came in with radio. I can't make an engaging, rousing or oratorical speech . . . but I have a good radio voice, and now I can get my message across to [the public] without acquainting them with my lack of oratorical ability.[9]

Coolidge's Democratic opponent, John W. Davis, didn't fare so well. One observer noted that Davis "has a voice which to the direct auditor has that bell-like quality of his delightful rhetoric. Via radio, however, this muffles and fogs."[10] Davis saw a change coming in political oratory. He said that radio "will make the long speech impossible or inadvisable . . . the short speech will be in vogue."[11]

In 1928, Democrats used radio to deliver an "all-star dramatization" of nominee Al Smith's life.[12] After defeating Smith, Herbert Hoover used radio extensively, but he wasn't very good at it. One critic said Hoover sounded like "an old-fashioned phonograph in need of winding."[13]

By 1936, Franklin Roosevelt was using radio as a principal campaign tool. His chief political strategist, James A. Farley, wrote that radio speeches were invaluable in counteracting negative newspaper coverage: "Yet no matter what was written or what was charged, the harmful effect was largely washed away as soon as the reassuring voice of the President of the United States started coming through the ether into the family living room."[14]

The emphasis in contemporary evaluations of radio in these campaigns—and a foreshadowing of things to come—was on voice, not content; on performance, not substance.

Roosevelt used a true ad on radio during his 1944 campaign. It included music, celebrity endorsements, and testimonials from members of the military and people who had benefitted from Democratic economic programs. In 1948, Harry Truman used similar ad formats.

Throughout these early years of broadcast advertising, the news media virtually ignored the content of politicians' spots. Ads were seen more as an entertaining diversion than as a substantive part of the campaign, and therefore were considered unworthy of press scrutiny.

Such judgments, however, were inconsistent with the simple mathematics of broadcasting's influence. For instance, William Jennings Bryan wrote that in his 1896 campaign he had traveled 18,000 miles through twenty-seven states and delivered 600 speeches in order to reach five million people. In the 1930s, Franklin Roosevelt reached sixty million Americans while sitting in the White House delivering a fireside chat.[15] When politicians use any medium that is this pervasive, their messages deserve close attention.

Considerable imagination went into the radio campaign designed to derail the writer and socialist reformer Upton Sinclair, who was running for governor of California in 1934. The main anti-Sinclair strategy was to scare voters about what would happen to their state if Sinclair won. Using the popular radio serial format, Sinclair's opponents created "Weary and Willie," two hoboes who were traveling across the country to California, where they would sponge off Sinclair's tax-funded welfare programs. Another serial, "The Bennetts," depicted a middle-class family discussing their lives and the campaign. One vignette: teenager Sis worries that she'll no longer be able to sing in her church choir during an atheistic Sinclair regime.[16]

Another campaign innovation to emerge from California campaigning—most notably in the 1934 governor's race—was use of the moving image as a political tool. Metro-Goldwyn-Mayer distributed five-minute shorts, "California Election News." Crafted to look like a nonpartisan newsreel, this actually was carefully designed anti-Sinclair propaganda. It included interviews of "typical voters," some of whom said nice things about Sinclair. But these pro-Sinclair speakers were strikingly unconvincing, and they were always followed by someone offering a more forceful anti-Sinclair view.[17]

Crude by today's standards, these shorts nevertheless established the campaign power of the moving picture accompanied by sound. They served as a preview of a future form of advertising, the television commercial.

Harry Truman and Thomas Dewey used television to speak to voters in 1948, but only about a million American households had TV sets then. By 1992, only about 2 million of the 94 million American households *didn't* have at least one TV set. In the interim—less than a half century—television had transformed American politics.

Beginning in 1952, presidential campaigns used TV ads. By 1960, almost 90 percent of American homes had television sets and, not coincidentally, 1960 saw the first presidential race in which television played a crucial, perhaps even determinative, role. The first televised presidential debate between John Kennedy and Richard Nixon was seen by an estimated 80 million Americans. The special impact of the medium was reflected in the response from the debate's audience: those who listened to the session on radio, thought Nixon had done better, while those who had watched it on TV—by far the larger number—thought Kennedy was the winner.[18]

These different judgments told politicians that from then on, not only would *what* they said be important, but also *how* they said it—or, more precisely, how they looked while saying it. Nixon's five o'clock shadow and his shifty eyes did more to hurt him than any policy position he took. Kennedy's "presidential" demeanor, on the other hand, helped him more than anything he said. That lesson has not been lost on candidates for all levels of political office.

Although 1960 may have been the breakthrough year for television's political influence, not until four years later did the full power of television advertising become apparent. The most dramatic example was a spot run by the Democrats. In it, a little girl stands in a field, picking petals off a daisy, counting them. When she reaches "nine," an adult male voice takes over, counting down from ten. The camera moves in tight on a freeze frame of the girl, ending up focused on her eye, which is looking pensively upward. After the voice reaches "zero," the screen fills with the image of a nuclear explosion. As the mushroom cloud takes shape, Lyndon Johnson's voice tells viewers: "These are the stakes—to make a world in which all God's children can live, or go into the dark. We must love each other, or we must die."

The name of Johnson's Republican opponent, Barry Goldwater, was not mentioned, but as Goldwater himself wrote about the ad, "There was no doubt as to the meaning: Barry Goldwater would blow up the world if he became president of the United States."[19] The Democrats, saying that they of course had not intended to sully Goldwater's character, withdrew it with great fanfare after running it once. (According to Bill Moyers, then a Johnson aide, it had been scheduled to run only once anyway.)[20]

News coverage of this ad was mostly limited to the protest raised by Republicans, who called it a "smear attack" on their nominee. Goldwater said the spot "completely misrepresented my position."[21] Given this furor, the press should have looked into the ad's content and Goldwater's public statements about using nuclear weapons, and then presented an independent analysis of the accuracy and fairness of the ad. But that kind of reporting was still years in the future.

The "daisy spot" was just one of many hard-hitting ads the Johnson campaign used in 1964. Others accused Goldwater—explicitly or implicitly—of wanting to destroy the Social Security system and poison children's ice cream with strontium 90 and other radioactive contaminants. To some extent, Goldwater had created his own problems with comments such as "Let's lob one into the men's room of the Kremlin," when discussing nuclear weapons. But regardless of Goldwater's self-induced difficulties, the nasty advertising of 1964 needed a referee. When public passions are being manipulated by politicians—through advertising or other means—reporters should dig out the truth.

Advertising in the 1968 presidential race must be judged in the context of that awful year. In the Vietnam War, the Communist forces' Tet Offensive further raised Americans' doubts about the purpose and winnability of that conflict. Martin Luther King, Jr., was assassinated, triggering disorders in several cities. Then Robert Kennedy was murdered the night he won the California primary. While the Democratic National Convention in Chicago nominated Hubert Humphrey, protesters outside the hall became victims of what investigators later called a "police riot." Alabama's George Wallace fueled his third-party presidential candidacy with thinly disguised racist appeals.

With all that going on, the country's mood was sour and voters' fears were ripe for being jabbed by advertisements. For instance, one Richard Nixon spot depicted a woman walking alone down an empty city street while the narrator says, "Crimes of violence in the United States have almost doubled in recent years. . . . And it will get worse unless we take the offensive. . . ."[22]

The purpose of this spot is not to stimulate thoughtful consideration of the crime problem but, rather, to scare the hell out of voters (much as Johnson's daisy ad was designed to do). Although the crime statistics in this Nixon ad may have been correct, such spots merit press scrutiny just to make sure the public realizes how the ad's makers are playing with viewers' emotions.

During the 1968 race, ads weren't analyzed that way. But this campaign did foster an important innovation in political journalism. A young reporter named Joe McGinniss was given remarkable access to the Nixon campaign staff and chronicled the cleverly manipulative use of advertising and other media techniques that helped win the White House.

This was McGinniss's premise:

Politics, in a sense, has always been a con game. The American voter . . . defends passionately the illusion that the men he chooses to lead him are of finer nature than he. It has been traditional that the successful politician honor this illusion. To succeed today, he must embellish it. Particularly if he wants to be President. . . . Style becomes substance. The medium is the massage and the masseur gets the votes.[23]

McGinniss's book recounts the day-to-day wheeling and dealing of Nixon's media advisers as they decided how to reshape the image of a candidate who had lost his last two campaigns (for president in 1960 and for governor of California in 1962). Their work is documented thoroughly in McGinniss's book; internal campaign memoranda offer fascinating insight into the cold-blooded navigating of the road to the White House.

The television strategists also had to redefine the relationship between the candidate and television, a medium that never had been kind to Nixon. These advisers, out of the sight of voters and most of the press, packaged and sold Richard Nixon. McGinniss accurately described the internal campaign dynamic vis-à-vis the public perception of the campaign:

The sophisticated candidate, while analyzing his own on-the-air technique as carefully as a golf pro studies his swing, will state frequently that there is no place for "public relations gimmicks" or "those show business guys" in his campaign. Most of the television men working for him will be unbothered by such remarks. They are willing to accept anonymity, even scorn, as long as the pay is good.[24]

McGinniss's exposure of this little-seen facet of campaigning was valuable, but his book wasn't published until after the election. His reporting provided the kind of information voters should have had *before* they decided how to cast their ballots. Journalists won't be able to uncover every bit of inside strategy; campaigners are protective of their secrets, and some of their machinations are neither important nor interesting. But because advertising is an essential element in campaigns, the McGinniss approach should be considered today when news organizations plan their coverage.

The Nixon campaign also showed how paid media may decrease a candidate's reliance on news coverage and drive a wedge between politicians and journalists.

Nixon's aloof unavailability to reporters, and his exploitation of television question and answer sessions beamed directly to the public, in which experienced reporters could play no part, as well as their sense that he was a "packaged candidate" being sold to the public like a marketable commodity, profoundly increased whatever dislike the press had held for him when his campaign began.[25]

In the following years, the art of political advertising became more refined, but news coverage of it changed little. Ronald Reagan's 1984 campaign ads set a new standard in production values. Aerial shots of the Grand Canyon and audience-grabbing use of color and music ensured an attentive audience. Soft-focus portraits of an idyllic, Norman Rockwell-like community illustrated the theme "It's morning again in America." The spots offered hope and reassurance,[26] making the case that all was right with the Reagan-led world.

These messages had been crafted not by the usual campaign advisers but by advertising professionals who had marketed Pepsi Cola and other consumer goods. Selling a candidate really doesn't differ much from selling a soft drink.

Reporters know this. They've known it for a long time, just as they've known that candidates wouldn't be spending millions on ads if they didn't influence voters. (In national campaigns, TV advertising is the largest item in candidates' budgets.) But until the 1988 George Bush versus Michael Dukakis race, little systematic effort was made to look at ads and their impact.

During the short span covering the 1988 presidential campaign, the 1990 congressional and state races, and the 1992 presidential contest, news analysis of campaign advertising changed substantially.

TRUTH TESTING

Is it true? That's the first question reporters should ask about a candidate's ad. Sometimes, if the ad relies on statements of fact (or purported fact), journalists can check the information and answer with a simple "yes" or "no." But outright lies are less common than exaggerations. Many politicians find safety in obfuscation; their "facts" are really opinions, dressed up to have the most impact on voters' thinking.

The standard format for newspaper truth tests is to present the verbatim text of the ad and critique either its line-by-line content or its overall message. The *New York Times*, for example, in its 1992 ad analyses described what appeared on the screen, identified the ad's producer, presented the verbatim script, addressed accuracy, and provided an overview scorecard.

For instance, late in the campaign the *Times* ran reporter Richard L. Berke's side-by-side critiques of Bush and Clinton ads. For the Bush spot, the "Accuracy" section began, "This ad is a case study in how accusations can be made and how facts can be used to bolster them or tear them down." The "Scorecard" began: "This ad takes facts out of context to paint Mr. Clinton as a governor who brought only misery to Arkansas. In reality, Mr. Clinton has been considered a better than average governor of a small, poor state." Within twenty-four hours, the Clinton campaign was airing a response ad, about which the *Times* said in its "Accuracy" section, "While the Bush ad makers selectively used figures to attack Mr. Clinton's record, this ad selectively uses figures to build up his record and makes assertions out of context." In the "Scorecard," the *Times* reported, "This ad inundates viewers with documentation to try to lessen the impact of one of the Bush campaign's harshest attacks."[27]

These critiques do not tell readers whom to believe or vote for. They are merely independent looks at highly partisan messages. A journalist's ethical responsibility includes giving news consumers enough information to make informed decisions. That's what these newspaper stories do.

Television journalists have a more difficult task when analyzing TV ads. One trap to be avoided is reinforcing a spurious message by rebroadcasting it. Sometimes candidates get more time and more credible exposure for their spots in news coverage than they get in the airtime they have purchased.

In fact, candidates have been known to produce an ad, unveil it at a news conference, wait for all or part of it to be shown on newscasts, and then not buy any airtime. If TV news organizations try to counter this maneuver by requiring that the ad actually be on the air before it becomes the subject of a news story, the campaign might respond by airing the spot on an obscure, inexpensive cable channel. The chess game continues.

If the video content of the ad is strong enough, viewers may focus on it, regardless of the reporter's narration. So even if the analyst is saying the ad's statements are lies, viewers might be so intent on the pictures that the candidate's message is reinforced.

Television journalists can respond to this in two ways:

— Not running the ad video full screen but squeezing it, usually into a graphic that looks like a television set. When coupled with an on-screen label saying "campaign commercial" or "ad analysis," this approach might jar the viewer into realizing that the ad content should not be looked upon as news or given the credibility of news. This is particularly important when the ad has been shot in a "news style," with use of sound bites and other editing techniques that make the ad look like part of a newscast.

— Forgetting subtlety and clearly labeling ad copy as untrue or misleading when that is the case. If, for example, a candidate falsely claims to be the only state official to have opposed an income tax increase, the ad should be frozen on the screen at that point, the ad analyst should say that this is not true, and the label "FALSE" should be imposed on the screen.

Candidates' advertising wizards often are smart enough not to make statements that can be clearly proven false. Many claims in ads are stated as fact but are really opinion. For instance, suppose an ad in a congressional race touts the candidate as "one of the most effective members of Congress," and cites no source of that rating. This shouldn't be denounced as false by the ad analyst because it is an opinion some people may agree with. But the analysis should underscore the absence of attribution and note other sources that disagree with the appraisal.

Such analysis might suffer a bit from its vagueness, but at least it lets some air out of the candidate's puffery.

News media scrutiny of candidates' ads hasn't brought total honesty to this aspect of campaigning, but it has made some politicians more careful about making false claims. According to *Newsweek*'s Jonathan Alter, the ad analyses "force campaigns to issue extensive documentation *before* the ad is aired—instead of waiting until the other side has complained. (By which point the ad has already done its damage.)" Alter also notes that the opposition might use the ad review as the substance of its *own* counterattack spot.[28]

At one point during the 1992 campaign, when many major news organizations were analyzing ads, the Bush campaign gave reporters thirty-five pages of documentation to back up one of its anti-Clinton spots, and the Clinton campaign quickly cranked out a seven-page rebuttal.[29]

Care should be taken when doing stories about ads. Calling a candidate a liar is a sure way to be accused of bias. News organizations should be certain to critique both sides' spots. But if one contender is more untruthful than the other, so be it. Howard Kurtz, who reported for the *Washington Post* about the presidential candidates' advertising in 1992, later wrote:

I felt a bit uneasy about criticizing the Bush ads more harshly than Clinton's ads, but the fact is that the Democrats, while occasionally shading the truth, were far more careful about documenting their charges. I was not going to equate jaywalking with bank robbery just to create an artificial "balance."[30]

Journalists have not relieved candidates of the responsibility to defend themselves. To win an election, when attacked, you must counterattack. In

1988, Michael Dukakis refused to do this. Four years later, Bill Clinton proved himself a master at it. The results of these two contests illustrate how important this skill is.

The news media's increasingly aggressive approach to campaign advertising is designed to benefit voters, not politicians. It provides a reality check—a few notes of truth amid the cacophony of exaggeration and lies.

THE FUTURE

Presumably, more news organizations will add campaign ad critiques to their political coverage repertoire. And certainly, candidates will be looking for new advertising avenues.

For instance, in states such as Florida, Texas, and California, where Spanish is spoken in many households, campaigners increasingly rely on Spanish-language television and radio outlets to deliver specially designed appeals. These ads should be analyzed not only by Latino news organizations but also by Anglo journalists. This means extra work, but the ethical responsibility to keep politicians honest transcends language differences.

Similarly, as cable channels proliferate, reporters must pay attention to other narrowly targeted appeals. As is already the case with radio, cable TV ads will be tailored to match interests of precisely defined audiences. Some politicians may be tempted to play on these groups' fears as well as their interests—for instance, about racial matters. News organizations should blow the whistle when such manipulation is discovered.

When journalists become more vigilant, politicians become more crafty. So reporters specializing in ad analyses must hone their expertise, studying nonpolitical commercials to learn tricks of the advertising trade, such as the effects of music, slow motion, subliminal messages, and other gimmicks.

Also, journalists must further examine their own role as referee. Just as reporters are ethically obligated to define limits about intruding into politicians' personal lives, so they should ponder the limits of fair play in candidates' attack advertising. An ad that truthfully denounces an opponent's public record is fine, but what about a spot based on court records of that same opponent's divorce ten years before? Should the press cry foul, or just let the voters decide on their own about the propriety of such tactics?

Ideally, ad critiques should be fully integrated into a news organization's political coverage plan, rather than being just an occasional sidebar. Advertising is too important in television-era campaigns to get anything less than thoughtful, well-researched coverage.

Chapter Six

Polls, Projections, and Endorsements

For journalists, the allure of public opinion polls is hard to resist.

Polls offer a crisp, quantitative portrait of a campaign. They reveal who's ahead, and sometimes why. They uncover voters' thoughts about candidates and issues. Best of all, for many reporters, the work is done by someone else; the numbers—with neat summaries and tables—are handed over to news organizations to use virtually verbatim if they so choose.

Because "much of political journalism is an artful effort to disguise prediction as reporting,"[1] opinion surveys are often relied upon as the principal basis for news stories. The theory behind this is that

Much of the reading and viewing public really doesn't care much about what happened yesterday in politics or in the campaign. Still less are voters enamored of weighty analyses of why something happened. What they want to know is: What's going to happen tomorrow? Who's going to win or lose? And if the reporter has even a vestige of conscience, he knows that this is the one question he can never answer with confidence.[2]

In the "horse race journalism" that so dominates much campaign coverage, polls often push aside stories addressing issues and candidates' fitness for office. Particularly as Election Day nears, poll stories develop a rhythm of their own—a drumbeat of increasingly dramatic intensity as the horses round the far turn and come into the home stretch. That rhythm can be hypnotic, entrancing journalists and their audiences. But it shouldn't be allowed to block out all else. As with other elements of campaign coverage, it should be kept in balance as part of a large and complex array of information.

Journalists may think that using poll data is a good substitute for their own guesswork. Maybe . . . but only maybe. Polls may have plenty of weaknesses that undermine their value as news. *Washington Post* ombuds-man Charles Seib urged journalists to challenge poll material: "[Pollsters] have sold us on the scientific validity of their business. . . . We fail to question the nonscientific judgments they make and some of the practices they engage in."[3]

Aside from the integrity of technical elements of survey research (dis-cussed later in this chapter), polls' significance should be evaluated dispas-sionately. Taking a poll is like taking a snapshot. Each provides an accurate picture, but only of what is happening at a particular time—the instant the camera clicks or the few hours or days when the survey is being conducted. Public opinion—like the subject of a photograph—is unlikely to remain static. Especially in the heat of a campaign, a major news story can cause rapid, dramatic shifts in opinion. So a poll can become obsolete hours after it has been taken.

Even absent any dramatic upheaval in a campaign, reporters shouldn't overestimate the importance of a poll. Despite the scientific precision of modern survey research, the poll is still someone else's work product. Even if it has been commissioned exclusively by the news organization, the news the poll contains has not been assembled firsthand by reporters.

Some distinction should be recognized between poll takers and news gatherers. "When the pollsters relay their findings to the public they become journalists—reporters of the public mood—but some of their prac-tices are journalistically questionable."[4] For example, the polling company might emphasize the most dramatic interpretations of findings or might fail to disclose all information about the sample, the questions, and other elements that could influence poll results.

The journalist—as the conduit between pollster and public—remains responsible for the integrity of the information that reaches the public. News organizations cannot ethically pass the buck.

As a general rule, opinion surveys should be seen as supplements to, not substitutes for, traditional reporting. They are best used as material to be included in larger stories, not as stories in and of themselves.

THE HISTORY AND NATURE OF POLLS

Some background about the evolution of polling will help in under-standing changing ethical demands. Journalists have had to keep up with increasingly sophisticated techniques of measuring public opinion. What had been a pseudoscience is now a respected research discipline.

George Gallup, one of the pioneers of opinion research, cites some key events in polling history:[5]

— In 1824, the *Harrisburg Pennsylvanian* and *Raleigh* (NC) *Star* published results of local straw polls that showed Andrew Jackson leading other presidential contenders. (Jackson, although he won a plurality of electoral votes, eventually was defeated by John Quincy Adams when the House of Representatives decided the outcome.)

— On Election Night, 1883, the *Boston Globe* sent reporters to check returns in selected bellwether precincts as a way to forecast final results. Versions of this approach are still used by news organizations.

— In 1912, several big city newspapers used personal canvassing to poll thirty-seven states.

— *The Literary Digest* began its polling in 1916, sending postcard questionnaires to its subscribers in five states.

— In 1932, *The Literary Digest* mailed poll "ballots" to 20 million households. About 3 million were returned. The magazine's final projection came within one percentage point of the actual results, as Franklin Roosevelt defeated Herbert Hoover.

— In 1936, *The Literary Digest* mailed its postcard ballots to a list of 10 million telephone users and automobile owners. The magazine confidently published the results: Alfred Landon, 57 percent; Franklin Roosevelt, 43 percent. When the real ballots were counted on Election Day, Roosevelt received 62 percent of the vote to Landon's 37 percent. This fiasco led to increased use of scientific selection, rather than massive mailings, to reach an appropriate sample.

— Despite use of better polling methods, 1948 was, according to George Gallup, "another crisis year in the history of polling." All the published polls forecast a victory for Thomas Dewey over Harry Truman.

— John Kennedy's 1960 campaign staff included pollster Louis Harris. In this run for the presidency, Harris polled more people throughout the country than any other analyst ever had done. "Upon his reports, upon his description of the profile of the country's thinking and prejudices as he found them, were to turn many of Kennedy's major decisions."[6] Harris's key role helped establish the practice of candidates hiring their own pollsters to aid in shaping strategy.

Looking back at the development of polling technology, Theodore H. White wrote that by 1980, "polls had become instruments of esoteric sophistication." The miscall of the 1948 Truman-Dewey race, he said, had been "the last major blunder of the polling men. They had since advanced from nose counters to analysts, senior strategists—experts in perception."[7]

The maturation continued. In 1992, six major media-sponsored polls all correctly projected the Clinton-Bush-Perot order of finish, most coming within a few percentage points of the actual vote.

Emerging from this checkered history is the fact that polls today—if correctly administered—are exceptionally accurate. But that "if" is very important. Failure, for instance, to sample "likely voters" instead of the general population can dramatically change the relationship of the poll data to the actual voting. (Only a minority of the general population casts ballots in most elections. Why poll nonvoters if you want to predict what will happen on Election Day?)

Before delivering poll results to the public, journalists should understand some of the basic elements of opinion research. Failure to know about such things makes the reporting of inaccurate or incomplete survey data much more likely.

First, the nature of a poll is determined by the kind of information sought. Among poll types are these:

— Candidate preference or "horse race." This is a staple of political coverage. Its basic question is something like "If the election were held today, would you vote for Bush or Clinton or Perot?"

— Performance rating. This is often used to measure opinion about incumbents. For example, "How would you rate Bill Clinton's job as president so far: excellent, good, fair, or poor?" Sometimes this may be more issue-specific: "How would you rate the way President Clinton is handling the economy?"

— Agenda setting. Politicians and journalists are always interested in learning what issues people think are important. This poll asks something like "Which of these issues do you think are important: jobs, the deficit, aid to Russia, gays in the military . . . ?" Further probing might be done with an open-ended question, such as "What do you think is the most important issue facing the country today?"

— Exit polling. This survey questions voters as they leave their polling places. It is considered highly reliable because voters are being questioned not about what they might do but what they have already done. Their answers about how they voted and why they did so are used in Election Night projections and analyses.

These poll formats lend themselves to infinite variations that can elicit deeper and broader responses. The validity of the data any poll produces depends largely on the quality of its design—its sample, its questions, and the way it is administered.

Flawed design is likely to mean flawed results. Sometimes defective polls are the product of sloppiness; sometimes a poll is skewed purposely. This might happen when, as a strategic ploy, a candidate wants to generate particular poll results for public consumption.

For instance, assume a Republican candidate believes she is trailing her Democratic opponent but wants the public to believe otherwise (perhaps to encourage contributors to her campaign). Her staff designs a candidate preference poll but selects the sample so Republicans are overrepresented. She'll probably fare quite well in that survey. Then she will release the poll results, along with the claim that they are "scientific proof" of the success of her campaign.

Similarly, a candidate's poll questions could be loaded to produce desired answers. Assume the politician in question wants evidence of public support for her proposed legislation limiting lobbyists' access to Congress. Suppose further that the poll question can be phrased in one of these two ways: "Do you favor restrictions on lobbyists' access to Congress?" or "Do you favor restrictions on lobbyists, who are trying improperly to influence legislation?"

The second question is sure to elicit more "yes" responses. When the candidate's pollster releases the survey results, however, the precise question may be omitted in favor of simply stating, "65 percent of respondents support the idea of limiting lobbyists' activity."

These are the kinds of gambits journalists must watch for. Before doing a story about either of these polls and presenting the numbers to the public, a reporter should ask about sampling procedure and question content. Failing to do so means ceding editorial control of the news product to the politicians.

Journalists aren't always passive recipients of rigged surveys. Sometimes they themselves are responsible for polls that have a good chance of producing slanted results.

For example, when presidential candidates Jimmy Carter and Ronald Reagan debated a week before the 1980 election, ABC, "with great fanfare, invited viewers to call in after the debate and report who they thought had won. Despite the fact that a less scientific poll could hardly be imagined, ABC still won a lot of attention for its announcement that Reagan had won by a two-to-one margin."[8]

Such ventures ask for abuse. Trying to create a bandwagon effect, one or both sides' partisans may engineer an organized effort to flood the "poll" sponsor with calls.

This "interactive" approach continues to be popular. CNN has invited its news audience "to glimpse a minute-long story, then dial an instant opinion."[9] In 1992, CBS urged viewers of the president's State of the Union address to participate in a phone-in poll. Further refinements in cable television technology will make such audience participation more common.

When such solicitations of opinion are undertaken, a crucial truth-in-packaging issue should be addressed. Clear distinction should be made between scientifically valid polls and the pseudo polls news organizations use mainly as an audience-grabbing gimmick. The latter should be accompanied by a disclaimer that stresses the unscientific way the sample was selected.

Or, to go a step further, a good argument can be made that any use of nonpolls should be dropped as being intrinsically deceptive. Despite disclaimers, many news consumers are likely to think a poll is a poll, and to give too much credence to survey results that lack scientific foundation.

EFFECTS OF POLLS ON NEWS COVERAGE AND VOTERS

Veteran campaign tactician Joseph Napolitan has said, "No one would base his campaign strategy on polls, but they are helpful in determining trends that can be acted upon. . . . Polls merely measure voter attitudes.

The use campaign directors and candidates make of that information is what is important."[10]

Journalists should adopt a similar perspective for looking at polls. Failure to do so may lead at least to weakened coverage and quite possibly to some ethical problems.

Individual reporters and news organizations collectively often become infatuated with polls—particularly those that they have commissioned, often at considerable cost. They can't resist flaunting their "exclusive *Daily Planet* poll." The mere fact that they have it is seen as justification for making its results the lead story—not just once, but headlining responses to different poll questions day after day.

The quality of information uncovered by the poll isn't of prime importance. Judgment about newsworthiness gets pushed aside in the giddiness that accompanies display of an exclusive product.

Also, news organizations sometimes let polls influence other coverage. In 1992, for example, when polls showed Clinton with a commanding lead, stories about him became a bit more upbeat and respectful, while Bush became the subject of many "poor George" stories.

Another part of polls' appeal is the ease with which survey results may be fashioned into a news story. A press release from a polling firm plus a summary of data requires just some editing and narrative to become ready for publication. Reporters, like most other people, aren't averse to occasionally finding an easy way to do their job.

Politicians sometimes worry that heavy coverage of polls may turn projections into self-fulfilling prophecies. For example, some of Walter Mondale's aides in the 1984 presidential campaign said that the constant flow of stories about Ronald Reagan's imposing lead in the polls early in the contest made it impossible for Democrats to convince voters that a competitive race was under way. The *Washington Post*'s David Broder acknowledged existence of this "battering-ram effect," but added that "generally, complaints about polls constitute a classic example of 'blaming the messenger.' "[11] After all, the polls did reflect the reality of Reagan's strength and Mondale's weakness in that campaign.

How a poll is interpreted can likewise produce controversy. In 1988, an ABC News/*Washington Post* poll just before the second Bush-Dukakis debate surveyed only 200 likely voters per state in all 50 states. As reported by ABC, the poll showed a huge Bush lead and influenced predebate news coverage that stressed the need for Dukakis to score a "knockout" if he was to have a chance of winning the election. The *Post*'s interpretation of the same poll's data was more conservative than ABC's; the newspaper put fifteen states in the toss-up category, while the network assigned that status to only seven states. Because the results according to ABC were more dramatic, they got the most attention from other news organizations (such as local media outlets).[12]

News stories frequently assign more meaning to polls than they deserve. For instance, surveys conducted by local pollsters in New Hampshire early in the 1992 presidential campaign "were routinely extrapolated by columnists and broadcasters to say something on a national level about one or another candidate's standing or future chances."[13] But New Hampshire voters' outlook may have little in common with that of voters in Illinois, California, Louisiana, or anywhere else. Journalists who overrated the New Hampshire poll results forgot to add an important ingredient to their reporting: logic.

Voters may be hypnotized by the weekly or even daily parade of poll numbers. Just as poll stories are easy for reporters to write, they are also easy for news consumers to digest, especially those news consumers who are paying only marginal attention to the campaign. They are particularly susceptible to being swept onto a poll-generated bandwagon, or caught up in a "consensus formation" effect.

Complexities of issues and nuances of leadership might be disregarded in favor of watching polls measure the progress of the horse race. Decisions about contributing to a campaign, volunteering to work for a candidate, and even voting are influenced by perceptions of "electability" shaped by poll results.

Even polls conducted at the same time and with similar samples can produce different results. When this happens, news consumers should be given the data from several sources so they can decide for themselves which information—if any—they want to believe. A news organization should not be so parochial that it presents results of only its own poll (unless other concurrent surveys have basically the same findings).

On one occasion in September 1992, a *Washington Post*-ABC News poll found Clinton leading Bush by twenty-one percentage points. The *Post*'s polling experts realized their results were out of line with other polls' findings—something that can happen as a function of sampling error. Nevertheless, the poll figures were proclaimed in a front-page headline. All previous horse race poll results had been carried inside the first section, including, the previous week, a poll showing Clinton slipping and Bush rising; the spread then was Clinton 51 percent to Bush 42 percent.

One ethical issue arising here is fairness. *Post* readers are likely to perceive a pro-Clinton bias in the way these two polls were covered. In both instances, the polls probably should have been reported several paragraphs into campaign stories. The twenty-one-point lead should not have been headlined. And since it was, some balance should have been introduced early on. Not until the story had jumped inside did a cautionary note appear: "The 21-point margin in the new *Post*-ABC poll is by far the largest of any recent public poll, and one the Bush camp sharply disputes."[14]

The volume of polling shows no sign of decreasing. In fact, news organizations are adopting methods that will give them even quicker measures of public opinion. In 1992, ABC, CNN, and even MTV used "instant response" polling to get moment-by-moment reactions of selected voters who were watching presidential debates. This allows an average citizen to beat postdebate pundits to the punch and, presumably, forces the pundits to consider the poll responses in their analyses.

Of course, speed has its price. On reflection, the debate watchers might change their minds about what they saw, so the instant-response poll should be treated carefully by its sponsor. The results certainly ought not to be used by sponsors to predict eventual voting behavior.

Part of the ethical dilemma surrounding such matters is rooted in the vague criteria for deciding how to use polls. At issue is not a clear-cut publish-or-don't-publish choice. Legitimate poll data are newsworthy and informative; news consumers deserve to see the survey results. Instead, questions concern *how* to publish: How much prominence should polls be given within overall political coverage?

Public concern about all this shows up in polls about polls. A 1988 Gallup survey found that

A large plurality of respondents resent the conclusion by news organizations and political analysts that a presidential race is essentially over when this "conclusion" is a mere projection based on inherently subjective data. Forty-seven percent of the public believes that reporting who is ahead in the polls does not improve press coverage. And 45 percent believes that such reporting is "a bad thing for the country."[15]

GUIDELINES FOR REPORTING POLL RESULTS

With so many polls available, and with their varied content and reliability, news organizations need consistent standards for determining when to pass poll results to the public.

The American Association of Public Opinion Research has a code of professional ethics and practices, and numerous news organizations have devised their own guidelines for polls. Among the key elements that should be known before publication are these:

— Who sponsored the poll

— When the poll was conducted

— Sample size

— How the sample was selected (e.g., registered voter lists, random telephone dialing, or some other method)

— Exact wording of the questions

— Raw number results (not just final percentages that may have merged or omitted categories such as "undecided" or "other")

— Statistical margin of error (which is a function of sample size).

These are important for the journalist evaluating the poll results and determining their news value. For instance, if the sample selection seems to draw heavily from population groups associated with one party, or if the questions are phrased to elicit predictable answers, the poll either shouldn't be reported or, if it is, it should be accompanied with a full explanation of its flaws. This should also be the procedure if some of the above-listed items aren't made available to the press. To do otherwise is to be left wide open to manipulation by politicians.

Further guidelines should address how polls are used. They should supplement, not lead, news reports. For example, a television news producer should not begin a newscast with "The latest poll shows Dan Quayle leading the Republican pack," and then back into a story about Quayle, the state of the campaign, or an issue. Do the substantive part first, then add material derived from the poll.

Also, journalists should keep in mind the inherent limitations of polls. Even surveys with good methodology can't reflect people changing their minds or withholding information. For example, in 1984, major news organizations' preprimary polling in New Hampshire showed Walter Mondale with a huge lead. But the polls, at least as reported to the public, didn't measure how soft that support was. This softness contributed to a massive last-minute shift from Mondale to Gary Hart.

Similarly, when a campaign incudes a very controversial candidate, such as former Klansman David Duke, some voters won't tell a pollster that they're voting for him.

Other unusual candidacies may affect polls' reliability. For instance, when Ross Perot ran for president in 1992, a significant part of his support may have come from people who had been so turned off by politics that they might not have voted or even registered in recent years. This may have left them outside the sample pool from which some polls picked their respondents. As it turned out, Perot's final vote total—19 percent—was several points higher than that projected by any of the major news organizations' polls.

Those surveys that are most reliable as bases for news stories are those measuring general attitudes about the state of the country or about issues. But even in these matters, polls often provide only superficial information about what people are thinking. Also, opinions can change quickly.

The principal guideline emerging from all these potential dangers is for the journalist to understand polling—to know what kind of information the survey was designed to find and to be able to judge if the poll was conducted fairly. Comprehending these things will help make polls and ethical journalism compatible.

ELECTION NIGHT PROJECTIONS

News coverage of Election Night is based on the premise that the public wants to know results as soon as possible. After many months of the horse race, the finish line finally has been reached.

As technology has advanced, so have news organizations' vote-projecting abilities. If all stops were pulled out, the major networks could give their audience a good idea of who will eventually win by midday, with the polls still open for many hours.

But what impact would such early reporting have on the rest of the day's voting? That question—to which there is no definitive answer—has fueled a long-running debate about the ethics of projecting election outcomes.

Presumably, people have been predicting voting results for as long as there have been elections. For most of that time, such prognosticating was based on instinct and guesswork. Because of the level of uncertainty, this was seen as harmless sport, taken no more seriously than calculating a bettor's odds for a sporting event.

But over the years, advances in polling have whittled away that uncertainty, making election predictions much more a sure bet than are tips about a thoroughbred race. And as Election Night became a television extravaganza, speed equaled—or perhaps surpassed—accuracy as the measure of the predictors' skill.

Television networks began making election predictions in their earliest days, the 1940s and 1950s. It was an imperfect science, as CBS and ABC learned on Election Night in 1960, when they pronounced Richard Nixon the winner, and then backed off when they realized how close the final results would be.[16]

The *New York Times* went through similar agony that night. Based on returns from eastern states, John Kennedy seemed to be doing extremely well; if the trend continued, his lead would be insurmountable. So, well before midnight, an early edition of the *Times* featured a huge page 1 banner headline: KENNEDY ELECTED PRESIDENT. Nixon, however, did unexpectedly well in midwestern and border states; although Kennedy still held a lead, his "trend" was fizzling and he seemed unable to reach an electoral vote majority. At about 2 A.M., another edition of the *Times* rolled off the presses with a new headline: KENNEDY APPARENTLY ELECTED.[17]

This caution was born of past embarrassments, most notably the 1948 headline on the *Chicago Daily Tribune* proclaiming DEWEY DEFEATS TRUMAN. Every journalist has seen the photograph of a grinning Harry Truman holding that newspaper aloft, and every journalist has had nightmares about making such a notorious mistake.

Beginning in the 1960s, the networks used analyses of key precincts as the basis for their projections. To do this, voting experts select several hundred precincts around the nation, each typical of a certain voting group (such as union members, African-Americans, or farmers). The analysts develop a "voting profile," based on past election performances, that illustrates how the precinct votes in a typical Democratic or Republican victory. On Election Night, returns from these targeted precincts are quickly reviewed to see if the vote is in line with past Democratic or Republican wins.[18] In 1980, for example, suppose in key precincts Jimmy Carter was found to be running well behind the totals he and other Democrats had won in previous elections. This would be a factor in projecting his eventual defeat.

During the 1970s, news organizations began relying on exit polls (discussed earlier in this chapter) as the principal basis for predicting outcomes. As numbers stream in, they eventually reach flood stage, inundating the audience—including other journalists—with voting research and actual voting returns and voting analyses. A member of the networks' audience, Theodore H. White, wrote, "We chew on this data; although we may not understand the algorithms of their election night projections, we usually accept them."[19]

At first glance, the ethical issue involved in all this is simply one of accuracy: make certain your projections have a solid, scientific foundation before presenting them to the public; don't become reckless in the quest to scoop your competitors. As an old wire service adage puts it, "Get it first, but first get it right."

Those are good rules, but much more is at stake. In Election Night procedures is found one of the most important questions in the ethics of political journalism: Should the journalist deliver news as promptly as possible to the public, or should news be briefly withheld if its early release might interfere with the political process?

The complexities of this question became obvious on Election Night 1980. The television networks projected early in the evening that Ronald Reagan would defeat Jimmy Carter. This was no surprise. Polls—including the candidates' own—had been showing that Carter was headed for a loss. But the networks' projections still influenced—not determined, but influenced—results of that day's elections.[20]

NBC projected Reagan the winner at 8:15 Eastern time; it flashed "Reagan Wins" at the bottom of the screen. At that time, voting was still going on in one-third of the states in the Central time zone and in every state farther west. In California, the polls would be open for almost three hours more. At 9:50 Eastern time, Carter made his concession speech, even though voting would continue in most Pacific time zone states for another hour or more.[21]

For Carter, the early projections and his statement made no difference; he was losing by a substantial margin. But some congressional and local races were much closer. They may have been affected by voters who decided, after hearing from journalists and the president, that they need not bother to vote. For example, two prominent Democratic members of

Congress—one from California and the other from Oregon—lost by narrow margins. Reportedly, lines of voters melted away after the network projection and Carter's concession.[22]

Postelection surveys of voters produced mixed results about the impact of early projections.[23] Not enough evidence exists to say with certainty that early projections and Carter's concession changed outcomes.

Over the years, studies have been inconclusive. A 1992 *New York Times* article noted, "The debate is largely driven by political lore, and the worriers are mostly Democrats, who tend to be less reliable voters than the generally older, richer and better educated supporters of Republicans."[24] Maybe so, but the research does at least suggest that the issue deserves more attention from news organizations.

In congressional testimony in 1981, William Leonard, then president of CBS News, said:

We believe our responsibility is . . . to report accurately the information we have, and its significance, as soon as it becomes available. . . . We cannot patronize our audience by withholding from them what we know. To do so would be a violation of trust and would seriously jeopardize our credibility.[25]

That has a touch of self-righteousness about it. News organizations regularly withhold information for ethical reasons when it might do more harm than good. For example, news of a kidnapping when publicity might endanger the victim, or reports about President George Bush's collapse in Japan in 1992 when details of his condition weren't known.

As one academic analyst of these issues in their political context has written, "Just as the media have the power to conduct exit polls and make early projections, they have the power not to do so if they desire."[26] Along the same lines, CBS commentator Eric Sevareid told a Harvard audience in 1984: "I never could understand the passion to know how people voted before the returns were in. Why can't we wait a couple of hours? I can wait. We've gone through a couple hundred years in this country waiting. It's not a strain on me."[27]

Another factor enters into journalists' Election Night behavior: common sense. In 1984, for example, anyone paying the slightest attention to the presidential campaign knew—as much as you can know anything about politics—that Ronald Reagan was going to pulverize Walter Mondale. The polls throughout the campaign showed a landslide on the way, and even Mondale's die-hard supporters knew they were going to lose. Once the early voting confirmed expected patterns, the eventual outcome was beyond any reasonable doubt. So if journalists on Election Night acted as if the outcome remained uncertain, were they being merely coy or outright deceptive?

The 1992 elections attracted 104 million voters to the polls and large audiences to their television sets. Combined ratings for ABC, CBS, NBC, and CNN were 46.3, compared with 34.8 in 1988. Even Comedy Central's live "Indecision '92" coverage got a .4 rating.[28]

During the early hours of coverage, network anchors seemed to be trying to build suspense as they urged their audience to vote. According to Elizabeth Kolbert in the *New York Times*, "Watching the network coverage of the election returns last night was like watching one long episode of 'I've Got a Secret.' "[29]

Because the networks had pooled their research resources, they were receiving most of their voting analysis at the same time. Yet the first proclamation of Bill Clinton's victory came not from the news media but from independent candidate Ross Perot in his concession speech at 10:30 Eastern time. The networks announced their projections of the final outcome about twenty minutes later, and soon thereafter carried the concession statements of George Bush and Dan Quayle. Clinton didn't appear before the crowd in Little Rock until after midnight Eastern time.

At first glance, it seemed that the networks had exercised commendable restraint. The *New York Times* editorialized that "the four networks deserve unstinting praise for threading a careful path between sensationalism and censorship." Writing in *Time* magazine, Michael Kinsley disagreed.

The drama that had you glued to your TV was a fraud perpetrated by a vast conspiracy [of journalists and politicians who knew exactly] what everyone else was waiting to hear, yet pretended ignorance. . . . . The networks generated false tension while suppressing the very information that would dissipate it.[30]

Kinsley argues that such restraint is misguided because by the time many West Coast voters are casting their ballots, the election *has* already been decided, regardless of whether the results are reported on television. He says early reporting has a negligible impact on results: "Why should knowing the outcome discourage voters for the loser more than voters for the winner, or vice versa?"[31]

Adding their voices to the discussion of this issue are organizations such as the Committee for the Study of the American Electorate, a nonpartisan research organization that purchased newspaper ads in 1992 urging the networks to change course. Among the arguments made in the ad was that "Early projections are bad journalism: The news on election night is the actual tally of the ballots cast. What the networks report on election night— projections based on their exit polls and/or sample precinct analyses—is not the news but their own contrivances."

The committee made the following suggestion:

There is a simple solution. The networks routinely withhold the results of sporting events to boost the ratings of their tape-delayed broadcasts. They voluntarily observe embargoes on news until specified times. And in 1988, the networks did not project the winner of the Canadian election, even though they had the capability to do so. The networks can simply voluntarily agree to stop projecting winners in races where people are still voting.

And so the debate continues. Journalists try to find the most ethical path through this maze. The search shows no signs of ending anytime soon.

ENDORSEMENTS

Standing in clear contrast to all the subtle ways in which the news media wield influence is the editorial endorsement, the news organization's official recommendation about how to vote. Nothing is shy about these pronouncements. The headline on the editorial (newspapers make most of the endorsements) will be something like "George Bush for President."

Despite this openness, ethical issues must be addressed. After designating a favored candidate or issue position, how can the news organization expect its readers to believe in its objectivity? Is the cost in public trust so high that endorsements should be abandoned?

For politicians, the value of endorsements varies. A well-established incumbent probably is helped little by such formal press support. But challengers welcome the added legitimacy an endorsement provides; they at least appear to have a chance of winning if news organizations think them worthy of endorsement.[32] Studies indicate that only a small number of voters are swayed by endorsements, and that independents—as opposed to party loyalists—tend to pay the most attention to them.[33] That means an endorsement might prove crucial in a close election.

Historically, Republicans have tended to garner the most endorsements because they are most likely to be favored by the news executives who determine editorial policy.[34] In presidential races, about 60 percent of America's daily newspapers usually endorse the Republican nominee, while 20 percent endorse the Democrat and 20 percent no one. From 1944 through 1988, the only Democratic nominee to receive a plurality of newspaper endorsements was Lyndon Johnson in 1964. In terms of circulation, the Republicans benefit even more: about 70 percent of the national daily newspaper audience reads newspapers endorsing Republicans.[35]

Effects of this Republican tilt are hard to evaluate. In 1976, for instance, if electoral votes for Gerald Ford and Jimmy Carter had been apportioned within the states based on the number of newspaper endorsements for each candidate, Ford would have received 538 and Carter 0. The actual vote was Carter 297 and Ford 240. Four years later, the hypothetical allocation based on endorsements would have given Ronald Reagan 444 to Carter's 46 (with 48 electoral votes in states where endorsements were evenly balanced). The actual totals were Reagan 489 and Carter 49.[36]

Although no hard-and-fast rule emerges from all this mathematical juggling, endorsements *can* matter, especially in races lower on the ballot in which many voters aren't familiar with the candidates. In such cases, the newspaper's recommendation is likely to carry more weight.

In all instances, several ethical imperatives should be observed. The first is to undertake the endorsement process conscientiously. *Washington Post* ombudsman Joann Byrd took a look at her newspaper's system shortly before the 1992 election. The editorial department, said its editor, Meg Greenfield, "is a bunch of nannies sticking our nose into everything. How, then, could we not tell you how to vote?" The *Post*, says Byrd, looks at more local than national elections, weighing in on races in the District of Columbia and its Virginia and Maryland suburbs. Editorial writer Robert Asher says choosing elections in which to make endorsements is similar to making judgments about which news stories to cover. With several hundred candidates and issues likely to be on area ballots in any given election year, the *Post*, says Asher, evaluates "importance, where change is afoot, what's at stake. We can't do all of them, and sometimes we think it's just best left to the community." When asked about how this system works, Asher answers, "We can never know enough; we hope it results in a fair portrayal."[37]

Another ethical requirement is to make certain that strict separation exists between editorial and news departments. The *Post*'s executive editor, Leonard Downie, Jr., in a 1992 column defined the problem: "Some readers are convinced that candidates endorsed by *The Post*'s editorial page are given more favorable news coverage. They believe that the entire newspaper wants these candidates to win." He states firmly that this is not the case, that the news department, which he heads, follows the paper's formal ethics policy: "On this newspaper, the separation of news columns from the editorial and opposite-editorial pages is solemn and complete." He underscores this:

Neither I nor any of the editors and reporters who cover the news under my direction has anything to do with these endorsement decisions or any of the other opinions expressed on the editorial page. Neither Miss Greenfield [the editorial page editor] nor any of the editorial writers has any involvement in our coverage of the news, including the election campaign.[38]

Responsible news organizations keep the wall between news and editorial functions in good repair. Despite this, a trend has emerged in recent years of newspapers backing away from endorsements. Columnist Richard Harwood refers to this as papers "depoliticizing themselves." Writing in October 1992, he noted that the *Baltimore Sun*, for example, hadn't endorsed a presidential candidate since 1980.

The *Sun*'s editorial page editor, Joseph L. R. Sterne, told readers: "No one needs our guidance. People can . . . make up their own minds." But the *Sun*'s reader representative, Ernest Imhoff, took issue with this: "Voters can't duck votes and editorial writers shouldn't duck such decisions." Jack

Rosenthal, who in 1992 was editor of the *New York Times*'s editorial page, agreed with Imhoff:

Newspapers tell readers every day what they ought to think about every issue under the sun. If they are going to assume the responsibility—and the arrogance and ambition—to want to call all the balls and strikes inning by inning [during a president's term] . . . don't they have the responsibility to add it all up at election time and give the final score?[39]

Rosenthal's position brings into focus another issue: backing away from controversy is not necessarily the way to move onto safe ethical ground. Ethics embraces participation—responsible activism that gives the public thoroughly considered opinion as well as thoroughly reported news. The key element in this is to make sure the audience will be able to distinguish between the two.

Chapter Seven

Covering the News Media

In the relationship between press and politics, the news media's power is always much in evidence. News coverage helps determine whether candidacies rise or fall, issues emerge or vanish, and policies succeed or fail.

This clout is respected, if not always appreciated or understood, by those who watch and participate in politics. It's accepted as part of the American political process. But if the news media police the campaigning and governing that make up this process, who polices the police?

This is not a new question. Although Plato, around 400 B.C., wrote, "it would be absurd that a Guardian should need to be guarded,"[1] few democratic political observers have been so sanguine. About 500 years after Plato's day, the Roman poet Juvenal asked, "Sed quis custodiet ipsos custodes?" Who is to watch over the watchmen?

That is a solid classical foundation for debate today. The press isn't shy about defining its own role as guardian. For example, the American Society of Newspaper Editors' Statement of Principles says the American press is supposed to "bring an independent scrutiny to bear on the forces of power in the society. . . ."[2] That refers mainly to government power, but presumably "forces of power" encompasses much more: big business, organized labor, education, the health care industry, and so on. Shouldn't the news media be ranked among those powerful forces?

Think about it: No other American institution of comparable power escapes press scrutiny. But for the most part, news organizations exempt themselves from the oversight they impose as a matter of course on their fellow power wielders. A few newspapers and magazines formally assign reporters to the press beat, and some of these journalists provide thoughtful critiques of how news organizations—including their own—serve the public. Others, unfortunately, detour into trivia; for example, some television critics prefer to relay gossip about sitcom stars rather than analyze news products.

Any institution—especially a powerful one—tends to go astray from time to time, purposely or accidentally misusing its authority. That's why oversight is important: to give an occasional tug on the reins. Usually a gentle pull is all that's needed.

The press does this regularly when others' behavior is the issue. For example, an officeholder who breaks a campaign promise can count on reporters telling the public about it. That's in keeping with the adversarial relationship between journalists and politicians. But that arms-length buffer doesn't exist when you cover yourself. Conflicts of interest abound; independence is hard to maintain.

Nevertheless, the job must be done. For one thing, public faith in the news media is unlikely to be maintained if the press is perceived as a rogue elephant, trampling on whomever it wants, whenever it wants. In 1947, the Commission on Freedom of the Press recommended that "the members of the press engage in vigorous mutual criticism. . . . If the press is to be accountable—and it must be if it is to remain free—its members must discipline one another by the only means they have available, namely, public criticism."[3]

Such criticism has appeared inconsistently, but frequently enough to have established a tradition of sorts. Noteworthy examples include a 1920 article in *The New Republic* by Walter Lippmann and Charles Merz that ripped the *New York Times* for systematically biased and incomplete reporting about the Russian Revolution. For example, they found in a thirty-six-month period of coverage nearly 100 occasions on which the *Times* erroneously reported that the Bolshevik regime was about to collapse.[4]

More recent press criticism has focused not just on story content but also on journalistic practices. For example, in 1972, *Washington Post* executive editor Ben Bradlee wrote a column explaining and critiquing what he called "a conspiracy in restraint of truth"—granting government officials anonymity in exchange for carefully selected "background" information. Background briefings, says Bradlee, are seductive for a number of reasons: journalists are apparently receiving confidences from big shots; the sessions are convenient for the press, since the information is delivered by the source without reporters even having to ask for it; and they are useful to the government because they let the sources put the government's spin on the information.

This game is replete with nonsensical trappings: backgrounders are often made available to large numbers of reporters; sometimes other people are present; and the same information is often available with attribution. The biggest flaw, says Bradlee, is that the public isn't told—except in a vague way—how this manipulative game is played or who these sources are. "In the name of common sense," he asks, "who is kidding whom?

When is the thoughtful professional in government and in the press, each properly concerned with his own credibility gap, going to stop it?"[5]

Bradlee's column illustrates what journalists need to do, and the difficulties in doing it. Exposing an abuse of the public trust is one of the news media's principal callings. In this instance, readers are told how the government influences public opinion. But Bradlee's criticism can't be—and isn't—directed solely at the public officials who use backgrounders; he also exposes sloppy journalists.

That creates a potential conflict of interest. In this article, Bradlee doesn't seem to be pulling any punches. But news consumers are likely to be suspicious when the press covers the press. How much will be told? How unrestrained will criticism be? Will honesty prevail over self-interest?

MECHANISMS FOR COVERING THE NEWS MEDIA

To avoid real or perceived conflicts of interest, press critics' independence must be assured.

The trickiest situation is that of the in-house critic. If the person watching the watchdog is too persistent, he or she may get bitten. To protect against this, the critic should be given a clear mandate and job security. For example, one early *Washington Post* ombudsman became the newspaper's only employee with a five-year guaranteed contract. If he so displeased his bosses that they wanted to get rid of him, they'd have to pay him for a portion of the remaining time. This allowed him to criticize even the *Post*'s top management without having to self-censor his comments.

In 1970, the *Post* designated its first ombudsman (a Scandinavian term referring originally to a government official who investigates citizen complaints about the government). The job involves a number of tasks: monitoring the paper daily and writing critiques for the benefit of editors and reporters; dealing with complaints from readers; and writing a regular column about the working of the *Post* and the news business generally.[6] The *Post*'s ombudsmen have been chosen from the ranks of journalism, academia, and government.

At least as rare as the ombudsman (who is found at only a few dozen news organizations) is the columnist or critic whose responsibility is more traditional. Rather than being the focal point for reader complaints or providing in-house critiques, these are basically reporters with the news media as their beat. They may write opinion pieces, but they'll also cover straight news; for instance, mergers between news organizations, relations between government and press, politicians' efforts to manipulate coverage, television news organizations' ratings-getting efforts, and so on. Lots is always going on in the news business, much of it primarily of interest only to the profession's insiders. But much also is significant to news consumers who want to know about the making of the news products on which they rely.

Another self-policing mechanism is the news council. This body is not formally attached to any news organization but sits as an independent monitor of press performance and an arbitrator of disputes between news media and news consumers. Its members may include academics, judges, and retired journalists, and its funding may come from news organizations and foundations.

Such councils have operated on national, state, and local levels. The basic process is simple: an individual or group that feels wronged by news coverage complains to the council, which then investigates and releases its findings for public consumption. It has no formal power, but it can shine a spotlight on controversies involving the news media.

The National News Council was founded in 1973, during the tense Watergate years when the Federal Communications Commission was beginning to investigate cross-ownership of news organizations. During its eleven years of existence, this council heard sixty-four cases and, at the request of individual publishers, issued forty-five statements supporting press freedom. In some of its findings, the council encouraged syndicated columnists to disclose conflicts of interest, upheld the right of free expression in one-sided columns, supported news organizations' efforts to get access to government records, and recommended ways to improve White House news conferences.[7]

One difficulty with this process is the lack of consistent visibility. For example, the National News Council's findings would be available for public dissemination, but they usually ended up being published in the *Columbia Journalism Review*, a respected publication but one with a relatively small audience composed mostly of people in the business. The general public wasn't being reached consistently.

Although some state and local councils survive, the National News Council died in 1984, mainly because of news organizations' lack of interest in and support for its work. Also, some news executives opposed having the press open itself to a process where outsiders—however nonpartisan they might be—would determine what is socially responsible news gathering.

Such wariness is understandable, if not wholly logical. It is discouraging commentary about the value journalists place on responsible criticism of their profession.

David Shaw, a *Los Angeles Times* media critic, says there remains "little systematic examination in the media of how the media do their job, what their decision-making processes are, what their traditions, limitations, objectives and profit margins are." A reason for this, says Shaw, is that "many news media executives are still hostile to criticism, from within and without, and most still seem to regard the internal workings of their organizations as either an arcane trade secret that the public wouldn't understand or as a sensitive state secret that's none of the public's damned business."[8]

Those attitudes haven't meant that news organizations escape scrutiny. In recent years, the work of the news councils has been supplemented or superseded by private watchdog groups. These organizations profess to be independent monitors of news organizations, but they often are partisan; their critiques of coverage reflect their vested interests.

Among these groups are Accuracy in Media (AIM), Fairness and Accuracy in Reporting (FAIR), the Media Research Center, and the Center for Media and Public Affairs. Of these, the *Los Angeles Times's* David Shaw writes, "The very existence—and virulence—of their criticism has helped contribute to the perception that the media are more flawed than ever."[9]

These groups rarely are shy about presenting their views. For example, AIM purchased a large advertisement in the September 27, 1992, *New York Times* that was headlined "A MESSAGE TO THE TV NETWORKS FROM YOUR VIEWERS: WE'RE FED UP WITH NEGATIVE, ONE-SIDED, DISTORTED TV NEWS!" It included the following passages:

We're a group of Americans who are sick and tired of how you in Television News, especially the famous network anchors, are using slanted, biased, deceptive news in a blatant attempt to manipulate public opinion. . . . We're mad at the way you're trying to influence the election by making sure you always find something critical or negative to say about candidates you want to lose, and show candidates you want to win in a positive way. We call that electioneering instead of honest, fair reporting. . . . And we're mad as hell at the way you never stop finding fault with our country.

Most press monitoring efforts—in-house or outside—are aimed not only at directly influencing news media performance but also at shaping public opinion. With varying degrees of diligence, news organizations try to be responsive to their publics. Popular sentiment, however, often is so amorphous that it's hard to define exactly what the public wants. Letters to the editor and comments by interest groups get news managers' attention, but this input isn't always representative of the public at large.

Organizations such as the Times Mirror Center for the People and the Press frequently commission polls to measure attitudes about media performance, and these provide useful insight about coverage generally and reports about particular topics.

In late 1992, for example, the Times Mirror Center surveyed voters and journalists to get opinions about press performance. Not surprisingly, opinions diverged. While 80 percent of the news media sample rated the year's campaign coverage good or excellent, surveys of the public throughout the campaign found fewer than 60 percent of the respondents rating press coverage favorably. The survey of journalists found that they lauded press coverage generally despite their widespread belief that this coverage was having a negative impact on the Bush campaign.[10]

That dichotomy underscores the importance of journalists' conducting reality checks to remind themselves that the public they purportedly champion often is less than impressed by their champions' work.

PRACTICAL APPROACHES TO COVERING THE NEWS MEDIA

Even after recognizing the need to cover themselves, news organizations often stumble in the process of getting it done. As of 1993, according to David Shaw, "only about 30 of the nation's more than 1,500 daily newspapers have ombudsmen; perhaps half a dozen have reporters who write full time about their own profession. Television gives the news media even less coverage."[11]

The *Washington Post* is among the relatively few news organizations that make serious efforts to cover the profession. Since 1970, it's had a series of ombudsmen whose independence has been well protected. In addition (again as of 1993), they have a reporter, Howard Kurtz, assigned to the journalism beat, and Richard Harwood, one of their senior op ed columnists, writes frequently about news media issues.

As Kurtz says in his book, *Media Circus*, "To be a media reporter for one of the nation's biggest newspapers is to dwell in the belly of the beast."[12] Like other powerful institutions, the press is sensitive about how it is depicted. Kurtz notes that his job requires "constantly putting other journalists on the spot." They react in various ways: "Many are good-natured about finding themselves at the other end of the notebook, but a surprising number resort to brusque 'no comment' or 'you'll have to speak to my editor.' " Some refuse to talk to Kurtz at all.[13]

Kurtz's job is, simply put, to evaluate the news product on which so many people depend. "Unlike most institutions," he writes, "the press can be judged each day by its outpouring of words and images."[14]

Sometimes a certain ambivalence is evident in Kurtz's assessments. For example, during the 1992 presidential campaign, rumors surfaced about George Bush having committed adultery. Tabloids and television networks gave the story prominent play. In his *Post* story about this, Kurtz led with Bush's angry denial, but the story—sustained by lots of gossip and only the flimsiest corroboration—still was presented as "news." Kurtz says, "Once again, even though the press had absolutely no proof that the allegations were true, we could not take a head-in-the-sand approach to a seamy story that had been all over television."[15] In other words, maybe it wasn't true, but if it ran on TV, it was news.

While Kurtz's articles fall under the rubric of news, Richard Harwood's work on the op ed page is designated as opinion. That gives him a certain leeway; having met the truth-in-packaging standard, he can state *his* views rather than having to remain more the dispassionate observer.

For example, in his column published on Election Day, 1992, Harwood mused about the press watching the press:

We'll be involved in introspective exercises for months to come. Do the politicians and people still love us? Were we guilty, guilty, guilty of the usual crimes: bias, superficiality, myopia, sensationalism, mud-slinging? Did we neglect that sacred animal, The Issues, or even worse, not understand what the "issues" were?

Answering such questions, says Harwood, isn't easy:

We have no instruments or formulas to measure "influence," "bias" or the "subliminal impacts" of our work. We attempt to inform or redeem or propagandize the audiences out there. But since it is one-way communication, we do not know if they hear what we are saying in the way we wish them to hear it or whether, in any case, their behavior is affected. . . . So we ordinarily fly blind, functioning out of habit and tradition, tinkering from time to time with the old ways of doing things.[16]

That passage provides a good sense of the breadth, and the limitations, of Harwood's mandate. Much evaluation of how the news media do their job runs into the brick wall of uncertainty. Judgments about ways in which the public actually uses and reacts to the news must be based on speculation.

The classic examination of political journalists at work and play remains Tim Crouse's *The Boys on the Bus*. Although the 1972 McGovern vs. Nixon campaign now seems like ancient history (didn't Thucydides cover that one?), Crouse's portrait of the political press corps as institution remains instructive.

Not surprisingly, journalists were leery about being scrutinized even by one of their own. As he traveled with reporters, Crouse found hostility among his erstwhile colleagues: "My company was in no great demand, word having gotten around that I was researching an article on the press. Reporters snapped their notebooks shut when I drew near."[17]

Despite this resistance, Crouse was able to analyze in great detail the mechanisms of pack journalism: what motivates reporters, how they work, how they evaluate their own product, and how they see their role in the political process. He explains arcane matters such as the influence of the wire service reporters—journalists whose names are unknown to most Americans but who have tremendous impact as leaders of the pack.

Individually, each of these items is fairly narrow. But collectively they take on striking significance; the whole is greater than the sum of its parts. What emerges from Crouse's saga is a recognition of power—the power to characterize a campaign in a way that becomes widely accepted by the voting public, and thus inevitably influences electoral outcomes.

Politicians watch all this with a mix of bemusement, exasperation, and anger. They tend to respect reporters' clout, but they often are dismayed by the frequency of misinterpretation or outright error in reports about politics. Further, many skilled politicians become infuriated by what they see as press nonchalance about accuracy. Their attitude is basically this: "If we make a mistake in a speech or an advertisement, we get promptly and loudly upbraided by reporters. But if they screw up, usually nobody says anything."

Among the sharp critics is Jody Powell, who was Jimmy Carter's press secretary and went on to become a syndicated columnist and television commentator. His general outlook on the news media is evidenced by the subtitle of his book, *The Other Side of the Story*: "When the news seemed to me, then and now, to be wrong, unsupportable, and unfair."

One of his premises is that

The major bias in journalism . . . the one most likely to promote deception and dishonesty, has its roots in economics. The fact is that news has to sell, or those who report it and edit it will find themselves searching for a new job. And that creates a bias to make news reports interesting. . . . If you want to get ahead, it is good to be accurate, but you had damn well better be interesting and salable.[18]

Powell also criticizes the press for being thin-skinned:

The fourth estate's hostile reaction to criticism, of virtually any sort from almost any quarter—and the corresponding lack of such criticism—is the most dangerous shortcoming because it, more than any other single factor, inhibits attempts to correct or at least alleviate all the other problems.

He suggests a remedy: "no-holds-barred, take-off-the-gloves competition similar to what exists in politics. If your competitor is a liar, or lazy, or cavalier with the truth, say so. If the opponent makes a serious mistake, pounce on it, tell the world about it."[19]

In other words, he wants the press to cover the press with the same fierce diligence that it brings to political reporting: "If the *New York Times* accuses someone of wrongdoing based on flimsy evidence, why shouldn't the *Washington Post* or the *Wall Street Journal* or the *Los Angeles Times* feel an obligation to check into the matter and, if need be, set the record straight?"[20] Because it lacks the fear of retribution such reporting would produce, says Powell, "journalism suffers by protecting rascals who ought to be ridden out of town on a rail."[21]

Powell's recommendation makes sense because it recognizes the parity of power between politicians and press. The determinative factor in deciding whether an institution should be covered and how aggressively it should be covered is how much power it has, whether it be formalized de jure power such as government wields, or de facto power such as the press possesses.

TELEVISION'S VACUUM

While the news media collectively may be hesitant to examine themselves too closely, television news has displayed even more reluctance about institutional introspection.

The principal rationale offered for this sluggishness is, in a word, "format." Television, so the argument goes, doesn't lend itself to devices available to the print media, such as "Letters to the Editor" columns, a regular place for corrections and clarifications, and opinion or analysis articles offering in-depth appraisals of press performance. Some exceptions exist. For example, CBS's "60 Minutes" makes a few minutes available each week for excerpts of viewers' letters, and ABC's "Nightline" occasionally focuses on press-related topics.

The problem isn't naïveté. TV news professionals know theirs is a medium particularly susceptible to politicians' exploitation and journalists' sloppiness. Kiku Adatto, a thoughtful observer of televised politics, writes:

Even as they tape the media events and show them on the evening news, however, television journalists acknowledge the danger of falling prey to manipulation, of becoming accessories to the candidates' stagecraft. One way of distancing themselves from the scenes they show is to turn to theater criticism, to comment on the scenes as a performance made for television, to lay bare the artifice behind the images.[22]

This means that rather than reporting about the journalistic process, some news organizations prefer merely to adjust their coverage of the politicians. This implicitly states, "Yes, we have been taken advantage of, but we'll counteract that by exposing those who would manipulate us." That should be done, but it avoids coming to grips with the structural flaws of TV news that foster the manipulation.

Fearing to jostle viewers by altering format, television executives claim to be prisoners of that format, blaming the intractable tastes of the public for the absence of innovation. "We're only doing what the public wants" is steeped in condescension and is a classic ethical cop-out.

This same excuse is frequently heard from television's entertainment programmers who say they provide trash because the public demands trash. That's outrageously self-serving. Of course, much of the public will watch whatever is provided. After ingesting years of brain-softening TV fare, many viewers may lack the will to demand better, or perhaps don't think that better is possible.

For the television industry, abandoning quality and diversity and slipping instead to the lowest common denominator is cheap, safe, and easy. But is it ethical?

TV news managers shouldn't have to ponder that question. Although non-news programming is pervasive and influential, journalism carries with it greater responsibilities than does entertainment. So, rather than claim enslavement to unchangeable format, the movers and shakers of TV news should devise ways to monitor themselves more effectively.

As a first step, basic information about the industry should be treated not as sacred mystery but as something viewers should know. For instance, the importance and measurement of ratings could be explained occasionally. Since so much of programming—news and entertainment—is driven by the quest for these numbers, the public should at least know what they are.

Also, television news should establish standard procedures for correcting and explaining erroneous or unclear reports. Why, for example, couldn't a network anchor end a newscast once a week by saying, "And finally tonight, we've received a lot of mail complaining about a story we ran last Monday, and we'd like to tell you how we went about reporting that story and give you some follow-up information."

This mission could be accomplished in two minutes. It might mean sacrificing a cute cat-up-a-tree feature story (much favored as an upbeat way to conclude a newscast), but it might also let viewers feel that the news process is something of a two-way street, that they are participants as well as recipients, and that if they take the trouble to comment about a story, they'll get a response.

Another way to open the TV news business to public scrutiny would be to devote an occasional program to explaining how it works—the decision making, the reporting, the technology, and so forth. As wedded as most Americans are to their TV watching, they might find fascinating an inside look at how those images get into their living room.

Also, thoughtful, balanced coverage should be given to the processes and impact of TV news. When, for instance, CBS and ABC refused to carry President Clinton's first prime-time news conference in 1993, those networks should have reported what they were doing and why, and included comments from a critic of their decision (preferably an independent analyst, not an administration spokesperson). Similarly, when campaign coverage is reduced to essentially a series of short sound bites and pictures of politician-produced media events, critics of that kind of journalism should be given a forum.

And when a network or station is guilty of an ethical lapse, not only should those involved come clean, but it should be reported by the competition, particularly if the public has a stake in the story. This was the case when NBC's "Dateline" rigged a test crash in a story about allegedly unsafe General Motors pickup trucks. NBC eventually apologized on "Dateline" and also reported the story on "NBC Nightly News." Because of the magnitude of this story (the interest of thousands of truck owners; GM's threatened lawsuit), other networks covered it as well. That was the right thing to do, but it was highly unusual.

Although the print media are far from perfect when it comes to self-examination, television still has a lot of catching up to do.

For individual or institution, introspection often is a painful process. The ethics of self-criticism require not merely openness but also willingness to correct failings when they are discovered.

The news media are not alone in their hesitancy to take on this task. Nevertheless, it needs to be done.

Chapter Eight

The Future . . . and Some Suggestions

As the preceding chapters illustrate, debate about ethics of political journalism is debate about power.

In wielding power, journalists act as analysts and referees, telling people not what to think but what to think about. That's generally accepted as being their job. But sometimes they themselves become players in the political drama of the moment. Their power pulls them to the center of things. When this happens, their role changes profoundly.

Because journalists' influence is so pervasive, they and the public they serve must possess some sense of what is and is not ethical. Otherwise, moral anarchy will wreck a democratic process that depends for its survival on the good faith of its participants.

At the heart of politics is the voter casting his or her ballot. That vote is based largely on the quality of information available about candidates and issues. More than any other source, the news media supply that information. If coverage is unfair or incomplete, the voter will be at a disadvantage, and the integrity of the political system will be undermined.

That's a weighty pronouncement, echoing the "good citizenship" sermons of the high school civics teacher. But that doesn't make it any less valid, and any journalist denying its truth is being disingenuous, if not irresponsible.

Like much else in this media-oriented era, politics is media-dependent. Politicians and journalists are locked in a symbiotic relationship that must remain in balance if their audience of news-consuming voters is to be properly served.

In this relationship, journalism should be driven by newsworthiness. Sensational "gotcha" stories are hard to resist, but they cheapen political discourse. Republican media guru Roger Ailes says:

Let's face it, there are three things the media are interested in: pictures, mistakes, and attacks. It's my orchestra-pit theory of politics. If you have two guys on a stage and one guy says, "I have a solution to the Middle East problem," and the other guy falls in the orchestra pit, who do you think is going to be on the evening news?[1]

Journalists seem increasingly ready to ascribe undue importance to a meaningless misstep or misstatement. For example, in a 1988 campaign speech, George Bush mistakenly referred to September 7, rather than December 7, as Pearl Harbor Day. It was an inconsequential error, but the network newscasts pounced on it. Dan Rather on CBS: "Bush's talk to audiences in Louisville was overshadowed by a strange happening." Tom Brokaw on NBC: "[Bush] departed from his prepared script and left his listeners mystified." Peter Jennings on ABC: "What's more likely to be remembered about today's speech is a slip of the tongue."[2]

Maybe it is more likely to be remembered, but only because TV news focused so intently on it. Bush wasn't babbling incoherently; he didn't say anything that revealed ignorance about policy. He made a minor mistake. It simply wasn't news until the anchormen made it news.

That these three networks all used the item says something about the collective mentality of TV journalists. It also illustrates the clout of network anchors—their ability to take a "news" item, no matter how inconsequential, wrap it in solemn phrasing, and present it to their audience as revealed wisdom.

This is just one facet of the news business. Ethical aspects of the anchor-centric nature of network and local television news deserve more attention. Anchors' big paychecks and celebrity status make them more like rock stars than journalists. They reach more people more often than presidents do; their bully pulpit at least matches that of the White House. Their utterances—whether they themselves or someone else writes them—can bring an issue out of obscurity. Their inflection can precipitate the rise or decline of a candidacy.

This is one of many manifestations of news media power. It should not be assumed to be malign; no evidence exists of anchor conspiracies. Nor should it be dismissed as being unworthy of persistent scrutiny. This much power—whether wielded by politician or journalist—should be treated warily. This will become increasingly important as more TV journalists make six- or even seven-figure salaries that will put them at a rarefied level far removed from that of the average news consumer.

Just as journalists' objectivity should be more closely monitored, so should their competence evolve to meet the changing demands of news technologies. Ever more emphasis is being placed on speed, sometimes at the expense of accuracy and sometimes with inadequate attention paid to the consequences of rapid-fire journalism. Typical of these matters are the science and ramifications of Election Night vote projections, addressed in Chapter 6.

The task for news professionals is to make sure their ethics keep abreast of the changing demands of their work. Leonard Downie, Jr., of the *Washington Post* has written that his newspaper's journalists are determined that news coverage—especially campaign coverage—will be "fair, unbiased and nonpartisan." He recognizes that this can be challenging:

Our determination may not always be clear to readers. Mistakes made in the rushed, highly imperfect process of churning out tens of thousands of words of news coverage on deadline every day can create unfairness that we try to correct over time. Language, especially in the few words of a headline, can convey unintended meanings. Aggressive reporting can be seen as crusading.[3]

Downie recognizes the importance of news consumers' perception of journalists' tactics and semantics. While meeting the public's standards of acceptable behavior in gathering and reporting the news, journalists shouldn't become gun-shy; they should remain aggressive, but ethically so. This means being alert, but not assuming that every statement from a politician or government official is untrue until proven otherwise. Former *Washington Post* correspondent Don Oberdorfer observes, "Without at least a modicum of trust on both sides, it is difficult to see how reporters and officials can relate effectively."[4]

Increasing coverage by CNN and C-SPAN, plus growing use of fax machines and computers, puts more pressure on editors and news directors to make snap decisions about the newsworthiness and accuracy of the deluge of information. Even governments look to TV screens as providers of up-to-the-minute intelligence reports. When Ted Turner and his colleagues claim "The world is watching CNN," they're right.

As Oberdorfer notes:

In some respects the biggest change in Washington journalism has been brought about by satellites, passing unseen in Earth's orbit. For the first time, news and pictures can be transmitted and received instantaneously nearly anywhere in the world. When dramatic events impend or occur, officialdom as well as journalists now watch in real time on satellite-connected media. This is a glorious technological triumph, but problems abound. What you see may not mean what you think it does; even events that appear to be unfolding before your eyes depend heavily on context for their meaning and interpretation. . . . There is demand for instant interpretation, which is often faulty interpretation, and for instant reaction, which may be panicky or misguided.[5]

Differences in coverage of the Vietnam and Persian Gulf wars show how dramatically technology can change journalism in less than two decades. Watching American bombs hit Baghdad . . . live; watching gas-masked journalists await Scud missiles in Israel . . . live; watching U.S. jets roar off on their missions . . . live. So much news to see. So much news to think about. So much news to evaluate and decide what it all means.

That leads to a crucial question: Has this surge of information produced a concomitant rise in knowledge? With an exotic smorgasbord of news laid out before us, are we as news consumers now able to cast wiser votes and make smarter decisions about varied aspects of our lives?

Answers to such questions hinge on the nature of the information that the public gets. John Taylor of *New York* magazine observes that CNN and C-SPAN have supplanted many traditional news gatherers.

Faced with a future of dwindling relevance, the print media, in particular, have developed coping or survival strategies. One has been to shift from news to analysis. Newspapers and magazines are increasingly devoted—in some cases over-de-voted—to packaging perceptions. At the same time, political talk shows, so cheap to produce, have proliferated. From all this flows perception competition, or Take Journalism. The endless commentary vastly exceeds the significance of the events usually under discussion. But, in a reworking of Parkinson's famous maxim, the news has been expanded to fill the space available.[6]

With 17,000 journalists permanently stationed in Washington, says Taylor, the shove and jostle of political perceptions can be fierce. "Prevailing opinions now have a shelf life shorter than that of fresh fish. No sooner are they established than they must be refuted."[7]

While the news business has been evolving, so have the ways politicians use the media to court voters. One big change that is still under way was evidenced in the 1992 presidential campaign: candidates' decreased reliance on "Old News" and their embrace of "New News." One appraisal of this shift notes that Old News consists primarily of

the "national" daily newspapers, the television networks, the news magazines and the wire services—those who have, quite literally, "mediated" between politicians and the public for decades. New News, by contrast, dispenses with mediation; it encompasses narrowcast cable TV, call-in shows, electronic town meetings, 800 telephone numbers, and all the rest of the targeted, direct-communications industry that technology has brought to America.[8]

As one acknowledgment of new electronic priorities, official White House documents are available to anyone on computer networks, and on the America Online service, the Clinton White House has its own e-mail address: "clinton pz."[9]

Having used New News successfully during his campaign, Bill Clinton saw no reason to abandon it when he moved into the White House. As Sidney Blumenthal observed in *The New Yorker* early in Clinton's tenure:

Policy and politics have merged: the Clinton administration is an accelerating political machine, geared to the passage of programs. Constituencies and legislators are targeted with precision, in media market after media market. Clinton's perpetual motion, his permanent campaign, is dictated, above all, by the system of checks and balances, which demands that he mobilize public pressures on legislators if he wishes to achieve anything. . . . Within each region, local radio stations, television stations, and newspapers are called daily to see if they'd be interested in an interview with an Administration figure.[10]

According to White House aide Jeff Eller, "We'd like to give the public a broader view, and put information into the hands of affiliate TV and let it decide what's relevant. You're giving more editorial empowerment to local TV as opposed to a desk assistant who's never been out of Manhattan. You're changing filters."[11]

This expanded access for local news organizations and reduced role for the traditional gatekeepers shifts some journalistic responsibility. If local journalists are to be principal intermediaries between president and public, they must take special care not to be manipulated. In particular, they should not be so concerned about protecting their newfound access that they become cheerleaders rather than reporters.

Many local print and electronic news organizations are up to the task. An example: In March 1993, Clinton met at the White House with thirteen journalists from southern Florida. They asked about Homestead Air Force base, Haitian refugees, Cuba, and other issues of particular interest to their audience. As Blumenthal notes: "These were not questions that the White House correspondents would be likely to ask: they were too detailed and narrow. But they were not 'softballs.' They were carefully and sometimes sharply posed."[12]

This is how the new system should work. The ethical requirement for local reporters will be to make a few adjustments in skills and standards to met the demands of national-level news gathering. That shouldn't be difficult.

Similarly, when candidates such as Ross Perot try to use the expanding variety of media vehicles to negate the news media's power as the voters' surrogate questioner, the press should be quick to let the public know what is going on. The notion of "town meetings" using interactive cable technology may prove to be a valuable enhancement of democracy. Or it may turn out to be a cynical perversion of democracy by asking voters loaded questions designed to produce the answers the meeting's sponsor wants.

Journalists should watch all this carefully. Ross Perot undoubtedly will not be the last politician to try to make press coverage irrelevant by buying massive non-news access to the electorate and by using other alternative media to evade reporters' scrutiny.

Even coverage of the more traditional elements of campaigning deserves a continuing ethics audit by journalists. As detailed in Chapters 3, 4, and 5, reporters' evaluations of candidates and their campaigns can easily be colored by arbitrariness and sensationalism. To avoid this, journalists need carefully considered, self-imposed guidelines—a mix of general principles and specific procedures.

For example, again consider the "character issue." In his book *Feeding Frenzy*, Larry Sabato presents a detailed "fairness doctrine" that defines which aspects of a politician's private life are legitimate subjects for news stories, and which ones deserve to be shielded from public scrutiny.

Journalists "ought to put more emphasis on *public* character than *private* character. . . . Part of the public side of character is on the record and easily accessible, such as courage demonstrated by taking issue stands that may be unpopular with the public-at-large or special interest groups. . . . The two most telltale indicators of public character are surprisingly little explored: how the candidate relates to his or her working associates and peers, and how he or she deals with staff.[13]

In addition to discussing the character issue, earlier chapters contain suggestions about refining day-to-day campaign coverage: keeping newsworthiness in mind while maintaining a frenzied schedule; using care when screening front-runners and also-rans in the horse race; determining exactly how far the "arms-length" distance should be between press and pols; avoiding too much reliance on media events and opinion polls; reporting about institutions as well as personalities; avoiding the conformity of pack journalism; testing the truth of campaign ads; and otherwise making sure that the campaign coverage reaching news consumers is fair, complete, and accurate.

How the news media do at these tasks affects the public's overall attitude about the political process. For example, writing about voters' dissatisfaction with both presidential nominees in 1976, *Washington Post* ombudsman Charles Seib noted:

The press cannot fulfill this desire for a charismatic leader by making Carter and Ford out to be more than they are. But a legitimate question is, are the practices and techniques of the news business making them appear to be lesser men than they are and the system more corrupt and ineffective than it is?[14]

Journalists should be careful not to let healthy skepticism be replaced by debilitating cynicism. Tough-minded reporting helps voters make informed appraisals of candidates and policies, but constant whining that "the sky is falling" alienates the public not just from politics but also from journalism.

Probably the most pronounced press bias isn't an ideological tilt but, rather, an antiestablishment and anti-incumbent prejudice. Beyond a certain point (which is hard to pinpoint), the watchdog's snarling produces diminishing returns. The public grows angry or bored; warning barks go unheeded.

Also, journalists can become so enamored of negative stories—the more salacious and apocalyptic, the better—that they can be suckered by those who peddle malice. Some stories have little significance beyond their nastiness, which usually is not the same thing as newsworthiness.

Reporters are particularly likely to slip into unrelieved negativism when they assume the role of theater critic, analyzing stagecraft more than substance. When story after story is about some form of manipulation, coverage takes on a sour taste. Certainly, politicians' efforts to con the public need to be exposed, but there is more to a campaign than this. Journalists have the responsibility to maintain a properly broad perspective.

Also, even while reporting about manipulation, reporters should be careful not to let their stories compound the problem. For example, in September 1988, NBC's Lisa Myers did a story about George Bush's television-oriented media events. But, says Kiku Adatto:

Even as Myers described the artifice of Bush's political theater, she provided additional airtime for some of his most flattering images. . . . Myers concluded by observing that the Bush campaign, by limiting reporters' access and "carefully scripting each event" was skillfully "managing the news." But in giving Bush's "carefully crafted images" another television run, her own report fell prey to the manipulation she documented.[15]

Another issue raised by this kind of reporting is perceived bias. Using pejorative terms such as "sound bites," "spin control," and "photo opportunities" is likely to be seen by some news consumers as a thinly disguised attack on the candidate who is the subject of the story. When such reports are done, journalists should be careful to treat opposing candidates as evenhandedly as possible. Of course, sometimes one side will be more enmeshed in political theatricality than the other, but often the story can be about not just George Bush's or Bill Clinton's campaign tactics, but also about the state of campaigning generally, offering examples of both candidates' less-than-honest courtship of voters.

Although journalists must tread carefully when preparing these reports, such stories definitely should be done. Voters deserve help when trying to see what's going on behind the smoke screens generated by campaigners.

But as appealing and useful as this rock-'em, sock-'em reporting may be, it should not supersede more stolid issues analyses. Over the long run, policies affecting health care, education, foreign policy, and the like will prove far more meaningful than will a politician's aptitude at campaign sleight of hand. This is yet another ethical responsibility: keeping in mind what is really important.

Making decisions about what the public needs to know (which often differs from what the public merely has a right to know) can affect a mammoth presence in American politics: the party of nonvoters, which in congressional election years can swell to about 120 million Americans of voting age.[16]

These people tend to be scornfully dismissed as the apathetic un-washed—people who care so little about their country or are so disdainful of things political that their electoral abstinence is a blessing. That, however, may be a simplistic diagnosis.

Writing in 1991, James Boylan, founding editor of the *Columbia Journalism Review*, raises this possibility:

Many members of the party of nonvoters are not irreversibly apathetic, cynical, ignorant, or self-indulgent. Many in fact may be making a political statement of their own—that they fail to see in current politics, as presented by the media, any connection between their vote and their political interests.[17]

The key phrase there is "as presented by the media." Perhaps in this television-dominated age the preeminent medium isn't presenting political news in a way that leads Americans to believe that they have a stake in such matters. Boylan continues: "It is probably more than a statistical curiosity that the three-decade decline in voting has coincided, almost to the year, with a similar proportionate lag in newspaper reading. Like voting, news-paper reading has become a more elite practice; in particular, the great cities are peopled with increasing numbers of nonvoters and nonreaders." While noting that there may not be a simple causal relationship between not reading and not voting, Boylan adds that "the two declines may share a common source—a lessening willingness by many Americans to consider themselves engaged in what, as recently as the 1960s, constituted a sense of common enterprise, that is, a national public life."[18]

Journalists certainly have good reason to object to disproportionate blame being dropped on them. The ills of American democracy have a complex root system; no single cause exists. But at the very least, journalism may be part of the problem and certainly could be part of the solution. By evidencing greater concern about engaging the public in politics, rather than implicitly encouraging people to sit by as passive observers, the press might stimulate participation. That means making sure that journalism does not remain, in Boylan's words, "like a panel discussion in which those in the audience never get to ask a question."[19]

As is discussed in Chapter 1, some news organizations are looking for new ways to engage their audience in the multistaged process that is journalism. Nothing is wrong with asking news consumers what issues they're interested in, how they prefer to have information presented to them, and just how important to them the journalists' priorities—such as speed and appealing pictures—really are.

Journalists who forswear "influencing the outcome" in politics are being foolishly disingenuous. They *do* affect results, so they should come to grips with the responsibilities this entails.

"Properly speaking, the American press *has* no ethics." That's the word from *Time*'s William Henry, one of the most thoughtful observers of the news media. "To do so," he says, "it would need a universally recognized and adopted code; journalists would have to agree to behave in a uniform and predictable way."[20]

As appealing as "having ethics" may be, a uniform code might not be such a good way to get them. Among reasons for caution are these:

— Any code applicable to news organizations of varied sizes and in different communities would probably be so general in its wording as to be virtually worthless. CBS News and the *East Wahoo Weekly Bugle* face vastly different ethical challenges; their scope of coverage and news-gathering techniques are very different. Also, a TV news operation must address some ethical questions, such as those related to live coverage, that are irrelevant to a weekly newspaper. Furthermore, the professional practices of the *Weekly Bugle* should reflect the community values of East Wahoo. Behavior of national or big city news organizations will be measured according to other standards.

— To have real meaning, ethical guidelines must have teeth. An individual news organization with its own code may devise ways to discipline violators. But who would enforce an industrywide code? Trying to set up an enforcement mechanism would open a debate about licensing and other bureaucratic controls. Such measures would be not only impractical but also almost certainly unconstitutional.

— Formal codes have less value than do training and journalistic practice rooted in ethics. Veteran newspaper editor Charles Seib observes: "I have come to the conclusion that while codes have some use as broad statements of standards and as prior restraints on disgraceful conduct and bases for action in response to such conduct, their natural resting place is the back of the desk drawer. I have never seen an editor faced by a real ethical-judgment call—Is this story an invasion of privacy? Did we make an adequate attempt to get and tell the other side? Is this headline or lead or page position misleading?—turn to a code or a set of rules for guidance."[21]

So if an all-encompassing code isn't realistic, what should be done? Certainly the absolute alternative—declaring ethical behavior unattainable—is unacceptable.

The answer might be found in a microcosmic approach. Rather than relying on the news business collectively to design and enforce ethical standards, the responsibility should be that of the individual journalist.

This is not an unattainable goal. Most journalists take their jobs seriously; they understand—at least vaguely—their societal role. Very few of them approach stories unethically—desiring to advance personal agendas or to use their power to conduct vendettas. Granted, sometimes they lapse into sloppiness or thoughtlessness, and in doing so may cause considerable damage. But this is correctable through *self*-discipline, *self*-policing.

The news industry and each news organization should do more to foster a professional environment in which ethical behavior is the norm. For example, the pursuit at any moral cost of sensational scoops should not be deemed praiseworthy, or even acceptable. Manipulation by politicians should be aggressively resisted. Those are among the profession-wide institutional principles that deserve adoption.

But on a day-to-day basis, when the news machine is running full tilt, all these matters become the province of individuals. Ultimately, decisions about ethics must be made by those men and women who travel on the bus, who dig through documents in the library and government archives, who put everything together in the control room and at the editor's desk—the men and women who say to the American people, "Here's the news."

Walter Lippmann's words serve as a fitting conclusion to this book's discussion of ethics and political journalism:

At its best the press is a servant and guardian of institutions; at its worst it is a means by which a few exploit social disorganization to their own ends. . . . The troubles of the press . . . go back to a common source: to the failure of self-governing people to transcend their casual experience and their prejudice, by inventing, creating, and organizing a machinery of knowledge.[22]

From that "machinery of knowledge" can emerge a thoughtful definition of news and a wise appreciation of the ramifications of news coverage. That is the foundation of ethics.

Notes

SERIES FOREWORD

1. See Robert E. Denton, Jr., *The Symbolic Dimensions of the American Presidency* (Prospect Heights, Ill.: Waveland Press, 1982); Robert E. Denton, Jr., and Gary Woodward, *Political Communication in America* (New York: Praeger, 1985, 2nd ed., 1990); Robert E. Denton, Jr., and Dan Hahn, *Presidential Communication* (New York: Praeger, 1986); and Robert E. Denton, Jr., *The Primetime Presidency of Ronald Reagan* (New York: Praeger, 1988).

2. Aristotle, *The Politics of Aristotle*, trans. Ernest Barker (New York: Oxford University Press, 1970), 5.

3. Aristotle, *Rhetoric*, trans. Rhys Roberts (New York: The Modern Library, 1954), 22.

4. Dan Nimmo and Keith Sanders, "Introduction: The Emergence of Political Communication as a Field," in *Handbook of Political Communication*, Dan Nimmo and Keith Sanders, ed. (Beverly Hills, Calif.: Sage, 1981), 11–36.

5. Ibid., 15.

6. Ibid., 17–27.

7. Keith Sanders, Lynda Kaid, and Dan Nimmo, eds. *Political Communication Yearbook: 1984* (Carbondale, Ill.: Southern Illinois University, 1985), 283–308.

8. Dan Nimmo and David Swanson, "The Field of Political Communication: Beyond the Voter Persuasion Paradigm" in *New Directions in Political Communication*, David Swanson and Dan Nimmo, eds. (Beverly Hills, Calif.: Sage, 1990), 8.

9. Sanders, Kaid, and Nimmo, xiv.

10. Ibid., xiv.

11. Nimmo and Swanson, 11.

CHAPTER ONE

1. Elizabeth Kolbert, "Paper Adjusts Reporting by Asking Its Readers," *New York Times*, June 21, 1992, A20.

2. Ibid.

3. John Bare, "Case Study—Wichita and Charlotte: The Leap of a Passive Press to Activism," *Media Studies Journal* (Fall 1992):152.

4. Daniel Schorr, "Ten Days That Shook the White House," *Columbia Journalism Review* (July/August 1991):23.

5. Mickey Kaus, "Sound-bitten," *The New Republic* (October 26, 1992):16.

6. Horace Greeley, *Recollections of a Busy Life* (New York: J. B. Ford, 1868), 404.

7. Glyndon G. Van Deusen, *Horace Greeley: Nineteenth-Century Crusader* (Philadelphia: University of Pennsylvania Press, 1953), 281.

8. Ibid., 295.

9. Henry Luther Stoddard, *Horace Greeley: Printer, Editor, Crusader* (New York: G. P. Putnam's Sons, 1946), 309.

10. Van Deusen, *Horace Greeley*, 421.

11. W. A. Swanberg, *Citizen Hearst* (New York: Charles Scribner's Sons, 1961), 273.

12. Frank Luther Mott, *American Journalism* (New York: Macmillan, 1941), 527.

13. Swanberg, *Citizen Hearst*, 162.

14. Ibid., 163–164.

15. Ibid., 173.

16. Richard B. Kielbowicz, "The Media and Reform, 1900–1917," in *The Media in America*, W. David Sloan and James G. Stovall, eds. (Worthington, Ohio: Publishing Horizons, 1989), 272.

17. Tom Goldstein, ed., *Killing the Messenger* (New York: Columbia University Press, 1989), 57–60.

18. James Deakin, *Straight Stuff* (New York: William Morrow, 1984), 88.

19. Peter Wyden, *Bay of Pigs* (New York: Simon and Schuster, 1979), 155.

20. Turner Catledge, *My Life and the Times* (New York: Harper & Row, 1971), 264.

21. Barbara Matusow, *The Evening Stars* (New York: Ballantine Books, 1984), 55.

22. Michael Arlen, *Living-Room War* (New York: Viking, 1969), 14–15.

23. Richard Joslyn, *Mass Media and Elections* (Reading, Mass.: Addison-Wesley, 1984), 163.

24. Gerald R. Ford, *A Time to Heal* (New York: Harper & Row, 1979), 319.

25. Spiro T. Agnew, *Frankly Speaking* (Washington, D.C.: Public Affairs Press, 1970), 67.

26. Ibid., 70.

27. Ibid., 85.

28. Paul Taylor, *See How They Run* (New York: Alfred A. Knopf, 1990), 177.

CHAPTER TWO

1. Howard Kurtz, "Networks Stressed the Negative in Comments About Bush, Study Finds," *Washington Post*, November 15, 1992, A7.

2. Leonard Downie, Jr., "News and Opinion at the Post," *Washington Post*, October 18, 1992, C7.

3. Michael Kinsley, "Bias and Baloney," *Washington Post*, November 26, 1992, A29.

4. Howard Kurtz, "Asleep at the Wheel," *Washington Post Magazine*, November 29, 1992, 10.

5. Ibid., 25.

6. Theodore H. White, *The Making of the President 1960* (New York: Atheneum, 1961), vii.

7. Jonathan Yardley, "Campaign '92: Can We Talk?" *Washington Post*, October 12, 1992, D2.

8. Haynes Johnson, "The Press: A Lack of Vigor," *Washington Post*, June 24, 1973, C1.

9. Walter Lippmann, *Public Opinion* (New York: Free Press, 1965), 226.

10. Ibid.

11. Timothy Crouse, *The Boys on the Bus* (New York: Random House, 1973), 266.

12. Ibid.

CHAPTER THREE

1. Gail Sheehy, *Character* (New York: William Morrow, 1988), 12.

2. David Cushman Coyle, *Ordeal of the Presidency* (Washington, D.C.: Public Affairs Press, 1960), 29.

3. Charles Dickens, *Martin Chuzzlewit* (Oxford: Oxford University Press, 1981), 256.

4. Kenneth W. Thompson, *Ten Presidents and the Press* (Washington, D.C.: University Press of America, 1983), 6.

5. Coyle, *Ordeal of the Presidency*, 362.

6. John B. Judis, "The Hart Affair," *Columbia Journalism Review* (July/August 1987:21.

7. Paul Taylor, *See How They Run* (New York: Alfred A. Knopf, 1990), 48.

8. Ibid., 52.

9. Ibid., 57.

10. "Private Life, Public Office," *Time* (May 18, 1987):33.

11. Ibid.

12. John B. Judis, "The Hart Affair," *Columbia Journalism Review* (July/August 1987):25.

13. P. Taylor, *See How They Run*, 77.

14. Ibid., 73.

15. Lawrence K. Altman, "Tsongas's Health: Privacy and the Public's Rights," *New York Times*, January 17, 1993, 16.

16. David S. Broder, *Behind the Front Page* (New York: Simon and Schuster, 1987), 99.

CHAPTER FOUR

1. Timothy Crouse, *The Boys on the Bus* (New York: Random House, 1973), 7.

2. Ibid., 8.

3. William A. Henry III, *Visions of America* (Boston: Atlantic Monthly Press, 1985), 76.

4. Mark Shields, *On the Campaign Trail* (Chapel Hill, N.C.: Algonquin Books of Chapel Hill, 1985), 24.

5. Roger Simon, *Road Show* (New York: Farrar Straus Giroux, 1990), 167.

6. Kiku Adatto, "The Incredible Shrinking Sound Bite," *The New Republic* (May 28, 1990):20.

7. Kiku Adatto, *Picture Perfect* (New York: Basic Books, 1993), 25.

8. Ibid., 67.

9. Adatto, "The Incredible Shrinking Sound Bite," 20.

10. Edwin Diamond, "Getting It Right," *New York* (November 2, 1992):18.

11. Alan L. Otten, "TV News Drops Kid-Glove Coverage of Election, Trading Staged Sound Bites for Hard Analysis," *Wall Street Journal*, October 12, 1992, A12.

12. Diamond, "Getting It Right," 18.

13. Richard L. Berke, "Clinton Bus Tour Woos and Wows Local Press," *New York Times*, August 9, 1992, 30.

14. Joe Klein, "On the Road Again," *Newsweek* (August 17, 1992):31.

15. Michael Kelly, "Democrats' Road Tour: Selling the Ticket Retail," *New York Times*, August 7, 1992, A14.

16. Leonard Downie, Jr., "Getting the Packwood Story," *Washington Post*, November 29, 1992, C7.

17. Nelson W. Polsby and Aaron Wildavsky, *Presidential Elections*, 6th ed. (New York: Scribners, 1984), 81.

18. Theodore H. White, *The Making of the President 1960* (New York: Atheneum, 1961), 368.

19. Ibid., 369.

20. David S. Broder, *Behind the Front Page* (New York: Simon and Schuster, 1987), 157.

21. White, *The Making of the President 1960*, 366.

22. Herbert G. Klein, *Making It Perfectly Clear* (New York: Doubleday, 1980), 85.

23. Howard Kurtz, *Media Circus* (New York: Times Books, 1993), 269.

24. Hedrick Smith, *The Power Game* (New York: Random House, 1988), 81.

25. Alexander Haig, *Caveat* (New York: Macmillan, 1984), 17.

26. Larry J. Sabato, *Feeding Frenzy* (New York: Free Press, 1991), 95.

27. Jody Powell, *The Other Side of the Story* (New York: Morrow, 1984), 253.

28. Sabato, *Feeding Frenzy*, 96.

29. Crouse, *The Boys on the Bus*, 216.

30. "Bushwacked," *Time* (February 8, 1988):19.

31. Joshua Meyrowitz, "The Press Rejects a Candidate," *Columbia Journalism Review* (March/April 1992):47.

32. Ibid., 48.

33. Broder, *Behind the Front Page*, 279.

34. Crouse, *The Boys on the Bus*, 342.

35. Bob Faw and Nancy Skelton, *Thunder in America* (Austin: Texas Monthly Press, 1986), 99.

36. Henry, *Visions of America*, 124.

37. Faw and Skelton, *Thunder in America*, 88.

38. Fred Barnes, "Jesse's Words," *The New Republic* (April 4, 1988):11–12.

39. D. D. Guttenplan, "Out of It," *Columbia Journalism Review* (July/August 1992):12.

40. Ernest R. May and Janet Fraser, eds., *Campaign '72: The Managers Speak* (Cambridge, Mass.: Harvard University Press, 1973), 97.

CHAPTER FIVE

1. Debra Gersh, "News Reports More Important Than Commercials," *Editor and Publisher* (October 31, 1992):23.

2. Lou Prato, "Selling Candidates and Selling Airtime," *Washington Journalism Review* (April 1992):54.

3. Kiku Adatto, "The Incredible Shrinking Sound Bite," *The New Republic* (May 28, 1990):21.

4. Mark Crispin Miller, "Political Ads: Decoding Hidden Messages," *Columbia Journalism Review* (January/February 1992):36.

5. Bill Monroe, "Covering the Real Campaign: TV Spots," *Washington Journalism Review* (October 1990):6.

6. Keith Melder, *Hail to the Candidate* (Washington, D.C.: Smithsonian Institution Press, 1992), 130.

7. Kathleen Hall Jamieson, *Packaging the Presidency* (New York: Oxford University Press, 1984), 23.

8. Ibid., 25.

9. Michael X. Delli Carpini, "Radio's Political Past," *Media Studies Journal* (Summer 1993):23.

10. Ibid., 25.

11. Ibid.

12. Jamieson, *Packaging the Presidency*, 25.

13. Delli Carpini, "Radio's Political Past," 28.

14. James A. Farley, *Behind the Ballots* (New York: Harcourt, Brace, 1938), 319.

15. Jamieson, *Packaging the Presidency*, 20.

16. Greg Mitchell, *The Campaign of the Century* (New York: Random House, 1992), 344.

17. Ibid., 371.

18. Tom Wicker, *One of Us* (New York: Random House, 1991), 228.

19. Barry M. Goldwater, *Goldwater* (New York: Doubleday, 1988), 198.

20. Merle Miller, *Lyndon* (New York: Putnam, 1980), 401.

21. Goldwater, *Goldwater*, 199.

22. Edwin Diamond and Stephen Bates, *The Spot* (Cambridge, Mass.: MIT Press, 1984), 168.

23. Joe McGinniss, *The Selling of the President 1968* (New York: Trident Press, 1969), 26, 30.

24. Ibid., 31.

25. Wicker, *One of Us*, 366.

26. Montague Kern, *30-Second Politics* (New York: Praeger, 1989), 80.

27. Richard L. Berke, "The Ad Campaign," *New York Times*, October 30, 1992, A19.

28. Jonathan Alter, "The Media Mud Squad," *Newsweek* (October 29, 1992):37.

29. Richard L. Berke, "Volleys of Data Replace Blatant Attacks of 1988," *New York Times*, October 29, 1992, A24.

30. Howard Kurtz, *Media Circus* (New York: Times Books, 1993), 299.

CHAPTER SIX

1. David S. Broder, "Political Reporters in Presidential Politics," in *Inside the System*, 3rd ed., Charles Peters and James Fallows, eds. (New York: Praeger, 1976), 218.

2. Ibid.

3. Charles B. Seib, "And the Pollsters Are Too Much with Us," *Washington Post*, October 22, 1976, A27.

4. Ibid.

5. George Gallup, *The Sophisticated Poll Watcher's Guide* (Princeton, N.J.: Princeton Opinion Press, 1972), 221.

6. Theodore H. White, *The Making of the President 1960* (New York: Atheneum, 1961), 56.

7. Theodore H. White, *America in Search of Itself* (New York: Harper & Row, 1982), 377.

8. Austin Ranney, *Channels of Power* (New York: Basic Books, 1983), 28.

9. Christopher Hitchens, "Voting in the Passive Voice," *Harper's* (April 1992):46.

10. Joseph Napolitan, *The Election Game* (New York: Doubleday, 1972), 136.

11. David S. Broder, *Behind the Front Page* (New York: Simon and Schuster, 1987), 296.

12. Michael Traugott, "Marketing the Presidency," *Gannett Center Journal* (Fall 1988):63.

13. Hitchens, "Voting in the Passive Voice," 48.

14. Joann Byrd, "The Endorsement," *Washington Post* October 4, 1992, C6.

15. Traugott, "Marketing the Presidency," 64.

16. Ranney, *Channels of Power*, 83.

17. Tom Wicker, *One of Us* (New York: Random House, 1991), 249.

18. Ranney, *Channels of Power*, 83.

19. White, *America in Search of Itself*, 186.

20. Peter Stoler, *The War Against the Press* (New York: Dodd, Mead, 1986), 160.

21. Ranney, *Channels of Power*, 84.

22. Ibid.

23. Percy H. Tannenbaum and Leslie J. Kostrich, *Turned-on TV/Turned-Off Voters* (Beverly Hills, Calif.: Sage, 1983), 60.

24. Jane Gross, "TV Projections," *New York Times*, October 29, 1992, A24.

25. Ranney, *Channels of Power*, 86.

26. Tannenbaum and Kostrich, *Turned-on TV/Turned-off Voters*, 209.

27. Broder, *Behind the Front Page*, 297.

28. Everette E. Dennis et al., *The Finish Line: Covering the Campaign's Final Days* (New York: Freedom Forum Media Studies Center, 1993), 29.

29. Ibid.

30. Michael Kinsley, "Election Day Fraud on Television," *Time* (November 23, 1992):84.

31. Ibid.

32. Charles Press and Kenneth VerBurg, *American Politicians and Journalists* (Glenview, Ill.: Scott, Foresman, 1988), 232.

33. Richard Joslyn, *Mass Media and Elections* (Reading, Mass.: Addison-Wesley, 1984), 238.

34. Nelson W. Polsby and Aaron Wildavsky, *Presidential Elections*, 6th ed. (New York: Scribner's, 1984), 72.

35. Joslyn, *Mass Media and Elections*, 150.

36. Polsby and Wildavsky, *Presidential Elections*, 72.

37. Byrd, "The Endorsement," C6.

38. Leonard Downie, Jr., "News and Opinion at the Post," *Washington Post*, October 18, 1992, C7.

39. Richard Harwood, "The Final Score," *Washington Post*, October 7, 1992, A25.

CHAPTER SEVEN

1. Plato, *The Republic* (London: Oxford University Press, 1945), 93.

2. James L. Hulteng, *Playing It Straight* (Chester, Conn.: Globe Pequot, 1981), 85.

3. Commission on Freedom of the Press, *A Free and Responsible Press* (Chicago: University of Chicago, 1947), 94.

4. Tom Goldstein, ed., *Killing the Messenger* (New York: Columbia University Press, 1989), 86.

5. Laura Longley Babb, ed., *Of the Press, by the Press, for the Press, and Others, Too* (Boston: Houghton Mifflin, 1976), 124.

6. Ibid., iv.

7. Robert A. Logan, "Jefferson's and Madison's Legacy: The Death of the National News Council," *Journal of Mass Media Ethics* (Fall/Winter 1985–1986):70.

8. David Shaw, "Media Credibility Shrinking," *Dallas Morning News*, June 20, 1993, J1.

9. Ibid.

10. Times Mirror Center for the People and the Press, "The Press and Campaign '92: A Self-Assessment," *Columbia Journalism Review* (March/April 1993):insert.

11. Shaw, "Media Credibility Shrinking," J1.

12. Howard Kurtz, *Media Circus* (New York: Times Books, 1993), 3.

13. Ibid., 4.

14. Ibid., 93.

15. Ibid., 292.

16. Richard Harwood, "Princes of the Tide," *Washington Post*, November 3, 1992, A19.

17. Timothy Crouse, *The Boys on the Bus* (New York: Random House, 1973), 12.

18. Jody Powell, *The Other Side of the Story* (New York: Morrow, 1984), 16.

19. Ibid., 293.

20. Ibid.

21. Ibid., 295.

22. Kiku Adatto, *Picture Perfect* (New York: Basic Books, 1993), 32.

CHAPTER EIGHT

1. Kiku Adatto, *Picture Perfect* (New York: Basic Books, 1993), 49.

2. Ibid., 48.

3. Leonard Downie, Jr., "News and Opinion at the Post," *Washington Post*, October 18, 1992, C7.

4. Don Oberdorfer, "Lies and Videotape," *Washington Post*, April 18, 1993, C1.

5. Ibid.

6. John Taylor, "Take Journalism," *New York* (April 26, 1993):10.

7. Ibid.

8. "Lexington," "Old News Locked out," *The Economist* (April 24, 1993):32.

9. Sidney Blumenthal, "The Syndicated Presidency," *The New Yorker* (April 5, 1993):44.

10. Ibid.

11. Ibid., 46.

12. Ibid., 45.

13. Larry J. Sabato, *Feeding Frenzy* (New York: Free Press, 1991), 221.

14. Charles B. Seib, "Voter Apathy: Is the Press at Fault?" *Washington Post*, September 17, 1976, A23.

15. Adatto, *Picture Perfect*, 33.

16. James Boylan, "Where Have All the People Gone," *Columbia Journalism Review* (May/June 1991):33.

17. Ibid.

18. Ibid.

19. Ibid., 35.

20. William A. Henry III,"Why Journalists Can't Wear White," *Media Studies Journal* (Fall 1992):28.

21. Charles B. Seib, "Ethics: Many Questions, Few Right or Wrong Answers," *Presstime* (February 1981):6.

22. Walter Lippmann, *Public Opinion* (New York: Free Press, 1965), 230.

Bibliography

Adatto, Kiku. "The Incredible Shrinking Sound Bite." *The New Republic* (May 28, 1990):20.
_____. *Picture Perfect*. New York: Basic Books, 1993.
Agnew, Spiro T. *Frankly Speaking*. Washington, D.C.: Public Affairs Press, 1970.
Alter, Jonathan. "The Media Mud Squad." *Newsweek* (October 29, 1992):37.
Altman, Lawrence K. "Tsongas's Health: Privacy and the Public's Rights." *New York Times*, January 17, 1993, 16.
Arlen, Michael. *The Camera Age*. New York: Farrar Straus Giroux, 1981.
_____. *Living-Room War*. New York: Viking, 1969.
Babb, Laura Longley, ed. *Of the Press, by the Press, for the Press, and Others, Too*. Boston: Houghton Mifflin, 1976.
Bagdikian, Ben. *The Effete Conspiracy*. New York: Harper & Row, 1972.
Bare, John. "Case Study—Wichita and Charlotte: The Leap of a Passive Press to Activism." *Media Studies Journal* (Fall 1992):149.
Barnes, Fred. "Jesse's Words." *The New Republic* (April 4, 1988):11.
_____. "Press Gang." *The New Republic* (June 21, 1993):15.
Bates, Stephen. "Political Ads: Journalists as Jurors." *The American Enterprise* (July/August 1990):15.
Bennett, W. Lance. *News: The Politics of Illusion*. New York: Longman, 1988.
Berke, Richard L. "The Ad Campaign." *New York Times*, October 30, 1992, A19.
_____. "Clinton Bus Tour Woos and Wows Local Press." *New York Times*, August 9, 1992, 30.
_____. "Volleys of Data Replace Blatant Attacks of 1988." *New York Times*, October 29, 1992, A24.
Blumenthal, Sidney. *The Permanent Campaign*. Boston: Beacon Press, 1980.
_____. "The Syndicated Presidency." *The New Yorker* (April 5, 1993):42.
Bode, Ken. "Pull the Plug." *The Quill* (March 1992):10.
Boylan, James. "Where Have All the People Gone." *Columbia Journalism Review* (May/June 1991):33.
Broder, David S. *Behind the Front Page*. New York: Simon and Schuster, 1987.

_____. "Political Reporters in Presidential Politics." In Charles Peters and James Fallows, eds., *Inside the System*, 3rd ed. New York: Praeger, 1976.

Byrd, Joann. "The Endorsement." *Washington Post*, October 18, 1992, C6.

_____. "Poll Play." *Washington Post*, October 4, 1992, C6.

Cannon, Lou. *Reagan*. New York: Putnam, 1982.

Catledge, Turner. *My Life and the Times*. New York: Harper & Row, 1971.

Coblentz, Edmond D., ed. *William Randolph Hearst: A Portrait in His Own Words*. New York: Simon and Schuster, 1952.

Commission on Freedom of the Press. *A Free and Responsible Press*. Chicago: University of Chicago, 1947.

Coyle, David Cushman. *Ordeal of the Presidency*. Washington, D.C.: Public Affairs Press, 1960.

Crouse, Timothy. *The Boys on the Bus*. New York: Random House, 1973.

Davis, Richard. *The Press and American Politics*. White Plains, N.Y.: Longman, 1992.

Deakin, James. *Straight Stuff*. New York: William Morrow, 1984.

Delli Carpini, Michael X. "Radio's Political Past." *Media Studies Journal* (Summer 1993):23.

Dennis, Everette E.; Adler, Wendy Zeligson; FitzSimon, Martha; Pavlik, John; Pease, Edward C.; Rogers, Deborah; Smillie,Dirk; and Thalhimer, Mark. *The Finish Line: Covering the Campaign's Final Days*. New York: Freedom Forum Media Studies Center, 1993.

Dennis, Everette E.; Adler, Wendy Zeligson; FitzSimon, Martha; Pavlik, John; Pease, Edward C.; Smillie, Dirk; and Thalhimer, Mark. *The Homestretch: New Politics. New Media. New Voters?* New York: Freedom Forum Media Studies Center, 1992.

Dennis, Everette E.; Adler, Wendy Zeligson; FitzSimon, Martha; Pavlik, John; Smillie, Dirk; Stebenne, David; and Thalhimer, Mark. *An Uncertain Season: Reporting in the Postprimary Period*. New York: Freedom Forum Media Studies Center, 1992.

Dennis, Everette E.; FitzSimon, Martha; Pavlik, John; Rachlin, Seth; Smillie, Dirk; Stebenne, David; and Thalhimer, Mark. *Covering the Presidential Primaries*. New York: Freedom Forum Media Studies Center, 1992.

Diamond, Edwin, and Bates, Stephen. *The Spot*. Cambridge, Mass.: MIT Press, 1984.

Dickens, Charles. *Martin Chuzzlewit*. Oxford: Oxford University Press, 1981.

Donovan, Robert J., and Scherer, Ray. *Unsilent Revolution*. New York: Cambridge University Press, 1992.

Downie, Leonard, Jr. "Getting the Packwood Story." *Washington Post*, November 29, 1992, C7.

_____. "News and Opinion at the Post." *Washington Post*, October 18, 1992, C7.

Elliott, Stuart. "Candidates' Spots Are Not Created Equal." *New York Times*, November 3, 1992, D18.

Epstein, Edward Jay. *News from Nowhere*. New York: Random House, 1973.

Farley, James A. *Behind the Ballots*. New York: Harcourt, Brace, 1938.

Faw, Bob, and Skelton, Nancy. *Thunder in America*. Austin: Texas Monthly Press, 1986.

Filler, Louis. *The Muckrakers*. University Park: Pennsylvania State University Press, 1976.

Ford, Gerald R. *A Time to Heal*. New York: Harper & Row, 1979.

Gallup, George. *The Sophisticated Poll Watcher's Guide*. Princeton, N.J.: Princeton Opinion Press, 1972.

Gans, Herbert J. *Deciding What's News*. New York: Vintage, 1980.

Garment, Suzanne. *Scandal*. New York: Anchor/Doubleday, 1992.

Gersh, Debra. "News Reports More Important Than Commercials." *Editor and Publisher* (October 31, 1992):23.

Gitlin, Todd. "Whiplash." *American Journalism Review* (April 1993):35.

Glaberson, William. "The Capital Press Versus the President."*New York Times*, June 17, 1993, A11.

Goldstein, Tom. *The News at Any Cost*. New York: Simon and Schuster, 1985.

———, ed. *Killing the Messenger*. New York: Columbia University Press, 1989.

Goldwater, Barry M. *Goldwater*. New York: Doubleday, 1988.

Graber, Doris. *Mass Media and American Politics*. Washington, D.C.: Congressional Quarterly Press, 1980.

Greeley, Horace. *Recollections of a Busy Life*. New York: J. B. Ford, 1868.

Gross, Jane. "TV Projections." *New York Times*, October 29, 1992, A24.

Guttenplan, D. D. "Out of It." *Columbia Journalism Review* (July/August 1992):10.

Haig, Alexander. *Caveat*. New York: Macmillan, 1984.

Hanson, Christopher. "Media Bashing." *Columbia Journalism Review* (November/December 1992):52.

Harrison, John M., and Stein, Harry H., eds. *Muckraking: Past, Present, and Future*. University Park: Pennsylvania State University Press, 1973.

Harwood, Richard. "The Final Score." *Washington Post*, October 7, 1992, A25.

———. "Princes of the Tide." *Washington Post*, November 3, 1992, A19.

———. "A Quick Peek at the Bush Diaries." *Washington Post*, January 23, 1993, A19.

Henry, William A. III. "Are the Media Too Liberal?" *Time* (October 19, 1992):46.

———. *Visions of America*. Boston: Atlantic Monthly Press, 1985.

———. "Why Journalists Can't Wear White." *Media Studies Journal* (Fall 1992):17.

Hertsgaard, Mark. *On Bended Knee*. New York: Farrar Straus Giroux, 1988.

Hinerfeld, Daniel Slocum. "How Political Ads Subtract." *Washington Monthly* (May 1990):12.

Hitchens, Christopher. "Voting in the Passive Voice." *Harper's* (April 1992):45.

Hulteng, John L. *The Messenger's Motives*. Englewood Cliffs, N.J.: Prentice-Hall, 1976.

———. *Playing It Straight*. Chester, Conn.: Globe Pequot, 1981.

Jamieson, Kathleen Hall. *Dirty Politics*. New York: Oxford University Press, 1992.

———. *Packaging the Presidency*. New York: Oxford University Press, 1984.

Jamieson, Kathleen Hall, and Campbell, Karlyn Kohrs. *The Interplay of Influence*, 3rd ed. Belmont, Calif.: Wadsworth, 1992.

Johnson, Haynes. "The Press: A Lack of Vigor." *Washington Post*, June 24, 1973, C1.

Joslyn, Richard. *Mass Media and Elections*. Reading, Mass.: Addison-Wesley, 1984.

Judis, John B. "The Hart Affair." *Columbia Journalism Review* (July/August 1987):21.

Kalb, Marvin. "Too Much Talk and Not Enough Action." *Washington Journalism Review* (September 1992):33.

Kaus, Mickey. "Sound-bitten." *The New Republic* (October 26, 1992):16.

Kelly, Michael. "Democrats' Road Tour: Selling the Ticket Retail." *New York Times*, August 7, 1992, A14.

Kern, Montague. *30-Second Politics*. New York: Praeger, 1989.

Kielbowicz, Richard B. "The Media and Reform, 1900–1917." In W. David Sloan and James G. Stovall, eds., *The Media in America*. Worthington, Ohio: Publishing Horizons, 1989.

Kinsley, Michael. "Bias and Baloney." *Washington Post*, November 26, 1992, A29.

———. "Election Day Fraud on Television." *Time* (November 23, 1992):84.

Klein, Herbert G. *Making It Perfectly Clear*. New York: Doubleday, 1980.

Klein, Joe. "On the Road Again." *Newsweek* (August 17, 1992):31.

Kolbert, Elizabeth. "For the Most Negative Ads, Turn on the Nearest Radio." *New York Times*, October 30, 1992, A19.

———. "Paper Adjusts Reporting by Asking Its Readers." *New York Times*, June 21, 1992, A20.

Kurtz, Howard. "Asleep at the Wheel." *Washington Post Magazine*, November 29, 1992, 10.

———. "Journalists on the Party Line." *Washington Post*, November 21, 1992, G1.

———. *Media Circus*. New York: Times Books, 1993.

———. "Media Circus." *Washington Post Magazine*, July 12, 1992, 19.

———. "Networks Stressed the Negative in Comments About Bush, Study Finds." *Washington Post*, November 15, 1992, A7.

———. "Sez Who? Sources and Reporters Play the Leak Game." *Washington Post*, March 7, 1993, C5.

———. "Who What When Where Why Be Objective? Politics and the Times." *Washington Post*, November 15, 1992, F1.

Leonard, Thomas C. *The Power of the Press*. New York: Oxford University Press, 1986.

"Lexington." "Old News Locked out." *The Economist* (April 24, 1993):32.

Lippmann, Walter. *Public Opinion*. New York: Free Press, 1965.

Logan, Robert A. "Jefferson's and Madison's Legacy: The Death of the National News Council." *Journal of Mass Media Ethics* (Fall/Winter 1985–1986):68.

McCubbins, Mathew D. *Under the Watchful Eye*. Washington, D.C.: Congressional Quarterly Press, 1992.

McCullough, David. *Truman*. New York: Simon and Schuster, 1992.

McGinniss, Joe. *The Selling of the President 1968*. New York: Trident Press, 1969.

Margolis, Jon. "Exit Polls and TV's Tyranny." *Dallas Morning News*, October 30, 1992, A29.

Mason, Todd. *Perot*. Homewood, Ill.: Dow Jones-Irwin, 1990.

Matusow, Barbara. *The Evening Stars*. New York: Ballantine Books, 1984.

May, Ernest R., and Fraser, Janet, eds. *Campaign '72: The Managers Speak*. Cambridge, Mass.: Harvard University Press, 1973.

Melder, Keith. *Hail to the Candidate*. Washington, D.C.: Smithsonian Institution Press, 1992.

Meyrowitz, Joshua. "The Press Rejects a Candidate." *Columbia Journalism Review* (March/April 1992):46.

Miller, Mark Crispin. "Political Ads: Decoding Hidden Messages." *Columbia Journalism Review* (January/February 1992):36.

Miller, Merle. *Lyndon*. New York: Putnam, 1980.

Mitchell, Greg. *The Campaign of the Century*. New York: Random House, 1992.

Monroe, Bill. "Covering the Real Campaign: TV Spots." *Washington Journalism Review* (October 1990):6.

Morrison, Donald, ed. *The Winning of the White House 1988*. New York: Time Books, 1988.

Mott, Frank Luther. *American Journalism*. New York: Macmillan, 1941.

Napolitan, Joseph. *The Election Game*. New York: Doubleday, 1972.

Novak, Viveca. "Who Decides Who's Serious?" *Washington Journalism Review* (June 1992):30.

Oberdorfer, Don. "Lies and Videotape." *Washington Post*, April 18, 1993, C1.

Otten, Alan L. "TV News Drops Kid-Glove Coverage of Election, Trading Staged Sound Bites for Hard Analysis." *Wall Street Journal*, October 12, 1992, A12.

Plato. *The Republic*. London: Oxford University Press, 1945.

Polsby, Nelson W., and Wildavsky, Aaron. *Presidential Elections*, 6th ed. New York: Scribner's, 1984.

Powell, Jody. *The Other Side of the Story*. New York: Morrow, 1984.

Prato, Lou. "Selling Candidates and Selling Airtime." *Washington Journalism Review* (April 1992):54.

Press, Charles, and VerBurg, Kenneth. *American Politicians and Journalists*. Glenview, Ill.: Scott, Foresman, 1988.

Quindlen, Anna. "Political Illiteracy." *New York Times*, June 6, 1993, E19.

Ranney, Austin. *Channels of Power*. New York: Basic Books, 1983.

Rossiter, Clinton, and Lare, James, eds. *The Essential Lippmann*. New York: Random House, 1963.

Sabato, Larry J. *Feeding Frenzy*. New York: Free Press, 1991.

Schorr, Daniel. "Ten Days That Shook the White House." *Columbia Journalism Review* (July/August 1991):21.

Schram, Martin. *The Great American Video Game*. New York: William Morrow, 1987.

_____. *Running for President 1976*. New York: Stein and Day, 1977.

Schudson, Michael. *Discovering the News*. New York: Basic Books, 1978.

Seib, Charles B. "And the Pollsters Are Too Much with Us." *Washington Post*, October 22, 1976, A27.

_____. "Ethics: Many Questions, Few Right or Wrong Answers." *Presstime* (February 1981):4.

_____. "Voter Apathy: Is the Press at Fault?" *Washington Post*, September 17, 1976, A23.

Seib, Philip. *Who's in Charge?* Dallas: Taylor Publishing, 1987.

Shaw, David. "Media Credibility Sinking." *Dallas Morning News*, June 20, 1993, J1.

Sheehy, Gail. *Character*. New York: William Morrow, 1988.

Shields, Mark. *On the Campaign Trail*. Chapel Hill, N.C.: Algonquin Books of Chapel Hill, 1985.

Simon, Roger. *Road Show*. New York: Farrar Straus Giroux, 1990.

Smith, Hedrick. *The Power Game*. New York: Random House, 1988.

Sparks, John. "Refereeing the TV Campaign." *Washington Journalism Review* (January/February 1991):23.

Stengel, Richard. "Bushwacked." *Time* (February 8, 1988):18.

Stewart, John G. *One Last Chance*. New York: Praeger, 1974.

Stoddard, Henry Luther. *Horace Greeley: Printer, Editor, Crusader.* New York: G. P. Putnam's Sons, 1946.

Stoler, Peter. *The War Against the Press.* New York: Dodd, Mead, 1986.

Swanberg, W. A. *Citizen Hearst.* New York: Charles Scribner's Sons, 1961.

Tannenbaum, Percy H., and Kostrich, Leslie J. *Turned-on TV/Turned-off Voters.* Beverly Hills, Calif.: Sage, 1983.

Taylor, John. "Take Journalism." *New York* (April 26, 1993):10.

Taylor, Paul. *See How They Run.* New York: Alfred A. Knopf, 1990.

Tebbel, John. *The Life and Good Times of William Randolph Hearst.* New York: E. P. Dutton, 1952.

Thompson, Kenneth W. *Ten Presidents and the Press.* Washington, D.C.: University Press of America, 1983.

Times Mirror Center for the People and the Press. "The Press and Campaign '92: A Self-Assessment." *Columbia Journalism Review* (March/April 1993):insert.

Traugott, Michael. "Marketing the Presidency." *Gannett Center Journal* (Fall 1988):57.

Troy, Gil. *See How They Ran.* New York: Free Press, 1991.

Van Deusen, Glyndon G. *Horace Greeley: Nineteenth-Century Crusader.* Philadelphia: University of Pennsylvania Press, 1953.

Wattenberg, Martin P. *The Decline of American Political Parties 1952–1988.* Cambridge, Mass.: Harvard University Press, 1990.

——— . *The Rise of Candidate-Centered Politics.* Cambridge, Mass.: Harvard University Press, 1991.

Westin, Av. *Newswatch.* New York: Simon and Schuster, 1982.

Whillock, Rita Kirk. *Political Empiricism.* New York: Praeger, 1991.

White, Theodore H. *America in Search of Itself.* New York: Harper & Row, 1982.

——— . *The Making of the President 1960.* New York: Atheneum, 1961.

——— . *The Making of the President 1964.* New York: Atheneum, 1965.

Wicker, Tom. *One of Us.* New York: Random House, 1991.

Wilson, James Q. "Stagestruck." *The New Republic* (June 21, 1993):30.

Wyckoff, Gene. *The Image Candidates.* New York: Macmillan, 1968.

Wyden, Peter. *Bay of Pigs.* New York: Simon and Schuster, 1979.

Yardley, Jonathan. "Campaign '92: Can We Talk?" *Washington Post*, October 12, 1992, D2.

Zoglin, Richard. "Stakeouts and Shouted Questions." *Time* (May 18, 1987):28.

Index

ABC, 4, 109–12, 114, 116, 130
Accuracy In Media (AIM), 125
Adams, John, 4, 95
Adams, John Quincy, 107
Adams, Samuel Hopkins, 13
Adatto, Kiku, 63, 94, 129, 139
Agnew, Spiro, 19–20
Agran, Larry, 80–81
Ailes, Roger, 6, 133
Alter, Jonathan, 102
American Association of Public Opinion Research, 112
American Journalism Review. See Washington Journalism Review
American Society of Newspaper Editors, 121
Anderson, John, 8
Arlen, Michael, 16–17
Asher, Robert, 119
Atwater, Lee, 6

Baker, James, 4
Baker, Ray Stannard, 13
Baltimore Sun, 119
Barnes, Fred, 86
Bay of Pigs, 15
Berke, Richard L., 101
Berra, Yogi, 81
bias, 21–24, 77, 138

Biden, Joe, 73
Blaine, James G., 46
Blumenthal, Sidney, 136–37
Bond, Rich, 23
Boston Globe, 107
Boylan, James, 140
Bradlee, Ben, 36, 122–23
Brinkley, David, 33
Broder, David, 28, 70, 110
Brokaw, Tom, 134
Brown, Jerry, 79
Browne, Malcolm, 15
Bryan, William Jennings, 96
Buchanan, Patrick, 23, 79
Burns, James MacGregor, 48
Bush, Barbara, 56
Bush, George, 4, 6, 7, 19, 20, 21–23, 25, 33–34, 37, 39, 42, 50, 52–53, 60, 63–64, 73, 76–77, 79–80, 82–83, 87–88, 101–2, 110–11, 116–18, 126, 134, 139
Bush, Neil, 56
Byrd, Joann, 119

Caro, Robert, 48
Carter, Billy, 56–57
Carter, Jimmy, 17–18, 22, 73, 82, 109, 115–16, 118, 128, 138
Castro, Fidel, 15
Catledge, Turner, 15

CBS, 109, 114, 116, 130
Center for Media and Public Affairs, 125
Charlotte Observer, 3
Chicago Daily Tribune, 114
Cleveland, Grover, 46
Clinton, Bill, 1, 3, 6, 7, 22, 25, 29, 39, 42, 49–56, 60–61, 66–67, 71, 79, 89, 101–3, 110–11, 117, 130, 136–37
Clinton, Chelsea, 56
Clinton, Hillary, 50, 55–56
CNN, 109, 112, 117, 135–36
Coleman, Milton, 86
Collier's, 13
Columbia Journalism Review, 124, 140
Comedy Central, 117
Commission on Freedom of the Press, 122
Committee for the Study of the American Electorate, 117
Connally, John, 80
Coolidge, Calvin, 95–96
Crenna, Richard, 39
Crouse, Tim, 28, 37, 60, 84, 127
C-SPAN, 135–36

"Dateline," 130
Davis, John W., 96
Deakin, James, 15
Dewey, Thomas, 30, 97, 107, 114
Dickens, Charles, 45
Dole, Bob, 73, 83
Donahue, Phil, 3, 33
Donaldson, Sam, 33
Dornan, Robert, 52
Downie, Leonard, Jr., 23, 68, 119, 135
Dukakis, Michael, 7, 19, 22, 29, 62–64, 73, 84, 86, 103, 110
Duke, David, 113

Eller, Jeff, 137
Exner, Judith Campbell, 47

Fairness and Accuracy in Reporting (FAIR), 125
Farley, James A., 96
Farrakhan, Louis, 86

Federal Communications Commission, 124
Ferraro, Geraldine, 56
Flowers, Gennifer, 3, 7, 49–51, 71
focus groups, 3–4
Ford, Gerald R., 17–18, 118, 138
Fortune, 46
Friedman, Steve, 64

Gallup, George, 106
General Motors, 130
Giancana, Sam, 47
Glenn, John, 60–61, 80
Goldwater, Barry, 98
Gonzalez, Henry B., 26
Gore, Al, 6, 34
Grant, Ulysses, 10
Greeley, Horace, 10–11
Greenfield, Meg, 119

Haig, Alexander, 72
Hall, Arsenio, 33
Harding, Warren, 95
Harkin, Tom, 55, 79
Harris, Louis, 107
Harrison, William Henry, 95
Hart, Gary, 42, 47–49, 54, 61, 80, 82, 113
Harwood, Richard, 119, 126–27
health of candidates, 55, 57
Hearst, William Randolph, 11–13
Henry, William A. III, 141
Hoover, Herbert, 96, 107
"horse race journalism," 77–78
Humphrey, Hubert, 99
Hussein, Saddam, 4

Imhoff, Ernest, 119
Iran-Contra scandal, 22, 31, 76–77

Jackson, Andrew, 44, 106–7
Jackson, Jesse, 85–87
Jefferson, Thomas, 44, 95
Jennings, Peter, 134
Johnson, Haynes, 35
Johnson, Lyndon B., 16, 79, 98, 118
Judis, John B., 48–49

Kaus, Mickey, 7
Kelly, Michael, 65
Kemp, Jack, 73
Kennedy, John F., 15–16, 46–47, 69–70, 98, 107, 114
Kennedy, Robert, 98
Kerrey, Bob, 55, 79
King, Larry, 32
King, Martin Luther, Jr., 98
Kinsley, Michael, 24, 117
Klein, Herbert G., 70
Klein, Joe, 65
Kolbert, Elizabeth, 3, 117
Kroft, Steve, 50
Kurds, 4
Kurtz, Howard, 26, 71, 102, 126–27

Landon, Alfred M., 107
leaks, 72–74
Leonard, William, 116
Libertarian Party, 8
Lincoln, Abraham, 10, 44, 95
Lippmann, Walter, 35, 122, 142
Literary Digest, 107
Los Angeles Times, 124–25

McCarthy, Colman, 81
McClure's, 13
McGinniss, Joe, 99–100
McGovern, George, 37, 82, 84, 88–89
Mackin, Catherine, 37
McKinley, William, 12, 95
Mattox, Jim, 43
Matusow, Barbara, 16
media events, 7, 18–19, 38, 62–65
Media Research Center, 125
Merz, Charles, 122
Miami Herald, 47
Miller, Mark Crispin, 94
Mondale, Walter, 19, 41, 60–61, 80, 110, 113, 116
Monroe, Bill, 94
Moyers, Bill, 98
MTV, 112
muckraking, 12–14
Murrow, Edward R., 16
Muskie, Edmund, 81–82
Myers, Lisa, 139

Napolitan, Joseph, 109
Nast, Thomas, 10
Natural Law Party, 9
NBC, 16, 37, 115–16, 130
The New Republic, 7, 86, 122
news councils, 124–25
Newsweek, 47, 50, 102
New York, 136
New York American, 11
New York Daily News, 17
The New Yorker, 16, 136
New York Journal, 11
New York Times, 15–16, 47, 80, 101, 114, 116–17, 122, 125
New York Tribune, 10
New York World, 11
"Nightline," 129
Nixon, Richard M., 17, 19–20, 28, 37, 47, 70, 75–76, 84, 98–100, 114

Oberdorfer, Don, 135
ombudsman, 123, 126
open meeting laws, 9
Otten, Alan, 64

pack journalism, 59–61, 127
Packwood, Bob, 68
Paine, Thomas, 44
Parker, Alton B., 11
Perot, Ross, 1, 6, 7–8, 9, 25, 30, 32–33, 39–40, 53–54, 76, 87–88, 91, 113, 117, 137
Persian Gulf War, 4, 135
political party reform, 88–89
Polsby, Nelson, 68
Powell, Jody, 73–74, 128
press bashing, 19–20
Pulitzer, Joseph, 11

Quayle, Dan, 20, 113, 117
Quayle, Marilyn, 23

Rather, Dan, 76–77, 134
Reagan, Ronald, 19, 41–42, 80, 100, 108, 110, 115–16, 118
Remington, Frederick, 11–12
Rice, Donna, 47–48, 54
Richards, Ann, 43

Robertson, Pat, 54, 83
Roosevelt, Franklin D., 15, 46, 96, 107
Roosevelt, Theodore, 12, 13–14, 95
Rosenthal, Jack, 120

Sabato, Larry, 138
Sasso, John, 73
savings-and-loan bailout, 26, 56
scheduling, 61–66
Schorr, Daniel, 4
screening process, 8–9, 78–81, 92
Seib, Charles B., 106, 138, 141
Sevareid, Eric, 116
Shaw, David, 124–26
Sheehy, Gail, 42, 57
Sinclair, Upton, 13, 97
"60 Minutes," 50, 129
Smith, Al, 96
Smith, Hedrick, 72
Socialist Worker Party, 9
socializing with politicians, 69–72
Spanish-American War, 11–12
Springfield Republican, 10
Steffens, Lincoln, 13
Stephanopoulos, George, 74
Sterne, Joseph L. R., 119
Swanberg, W. A., 11

talk shows, 23, 32–34, 53, 87, 136
Tarbell, Ida, 13
Taylor, John, 136
Taylor, Paul, 48

Thomas, Clarence, 37
Time, 50, 117
Times Mirror Center for the People
    and the Press, 91, 125
Truman, Harry, 30, 96, 107, 114
Tsongas, Paul, 55, 57, 79
Turner, Ted, 135
Tyler, John, 95

Van Buren, Martin, 95
Vander Jagt, Guy, 66–68
Vietnam War, 17, 47, 135
voting, by journalists, 23–24

Wallace, George, 8, 99
Washington, George, 43–44, 95
Washington Journalism Review, 50, 94
Washington Post, 23, 33, 36, 48, 50, 68,
    86, 102, 106, 110–11, 119, 122–23,
    126, 135
Watergate scandal, 17, 35, 47, 124
White, Theodore H., 27–28, 70, 107
Wichita Eagle, 3
Wildavsky, Aaron, 68
Williams, Clayton, 93
Wilson, Woodrow, 45–46

Yardley, Jonathan, 33

Zaccaro, John, 56
Ziegler, Ron, 75
Zirinsky, Susan, 64

About the Author

PHILIP SEIB is Associate Professor of Journalism at Southern Methodist University. He is also a columnist for the *Dallas Morning News* and is political analyst for the ABC-affiliate, WFAA Television, in Dallas. He is the author of five other books, including *Who's in Charge: How the Media Shape News and Politicians Win Votes* (1987).